£10

C000139345

The Tale of a

Church Planter

The Tale of a Church Planter

The ups, downs, frustrations, joys and everything in-between on the roller coaster ride of church planting.

ANGELA DE SOUZA

Copyright © 2012 by Angela De Souza

ALL RIGHTS RESERVED

No part of this book may be reproduced, stored in a retrieval system, or transmitted, in any form or by any means — electronic, mechanical, photocopying, recording or otherwise — without prior written permission.

ISBN-13:   978-1466484108

ISBN-10:   1466484101

BISAC: Religion / Christianity / General

*This book is dedicated to my God and King – WOW! I just never knew that **this** life was possible. Talk about a rollercoaster ride. What a thrill to be serving you. X*

To my wonderful husband and four gorgeous children -   thank you that we could be on this journey together, I don't take it for granted that we have built this church together – as a family ☺

To Dave, who would have thought that it would be possible to have such a good friend like you? You are amazing and the strong pillar of D7 Church.

Contents

Introduction

My name is Angela De Souza, I am the mother of four gorgeous children, Lorah-Kelly, Jordan, Daniel and Amy. My husband and I are the senior pastors of D7 Church and at the time of this writing I served in the capacity of Executive Pastor too.

I can honestly say that no recipe or formula for church building exists - God does not work in this way! D7 Church is living proof of this. Not because we didn't try, we did try, we tried just about everything.

Oswald Chambers writes, *"Never make a principle out of your experience, let God be as original with other people as He is with you."*[1] In the same way I would say, don't try and copy our journey or make principles out of our experiences, let God be as original with your church as He was with ours. We did not fit into a mould or a recipe, even though at first we tried to. Our bookshelf is lined with books that tell you what works and what doesn't work. Our computer is filled with files of blog posts from mega-church pastors and documents with strategy from other churches. We have attended conferences and visited all sorts of churches to try and learn about building a church.

It was only when we gave up and said so to God that we began to have breakthrough. This is our story. It was when we stopped trying to follow a formula and started to rely on the Holy Spirit that we truly saw God at work. This book is our story but that is all it is, nothing more. You will not find a formula or a strategy here; you will not find any 'how tos' or seven steps to achieve what you want. It was in our ignorance that God chose to move and in our utter dependence on Him that gave Him freedom to have His way. Nothing worked out as we had planned but everything turned out for the best.

Our story has been recorded to encourage you on your journey and to glorify God. It is His church and He will have His way *because the foolishness of God is wiser than men, and the weakness of God is stronger than men. For you see your calling, brethren, that not many wise according to the flesh, not many mighty, not many noble, are called. But God has chosen the foolish things of the world to put to shame the wise, and God has chosen the weak things of the world to put to shame the things which are mighty, and the base things of the world and the things which are despised God has chosen, and the things which are not, to bring to nothing the things that are, that no flesh should glory in His presence.*

-     *1 Corinthians 1:25-29*

Timeline

2006

Friday night youth group started in our home

Thursday night connect group started in our home

Our baby boy, Daniel, was born

2007

Kept on keeping on with our activities in our home

We bought our first house

We bought a reliable car after ours kept breaking down

2008

Moved youth group from home to Community Centre

Planted our church in Community Centre

Our baby girl, Amy, was born

2009 →

D7 Church was born

King's Daughters was born

2010 →

Recorded our first church CD, *King's Square*

2011 →

Recorded our second CD, *In the Stillness*

King's Daughters Conference was born

Began training a pastoral team

Started a second church service in Cheltenham

Launched the vision for D7 Arena

2012 →

The journey continues... in the next book, *The Tale of a Church Leader*

Chapter 1
In the Beginning

In the Beginning

It was the early spring of 2006. Lorah-Kelly, my eldest daughter, was fourteen years old. She had just started attending a new secondary school and her life was very unsettled.

Driving Lorah-Kelly and Jordan, my eleven-year-old daughter, to school each day, was really special as the Cotswolds were in full bloom and so very beautiful this time of year. Cheltenham, by comparison to London, from where we had moved, was breathtaking. We were enjoying our new home and our new life out in the country. Eric and I, along with our two daughters, had moved to Cheltenham to build a new life for ourselves. Although everything seemed to be going according to plan, we did have a slight issue in that the Cheltenham schools were oversubscribed and the nearest school with a vacancy was in the next city, Gloucester.

Lorah-Kelly had no option but to go to a Gloucester school, which didn't seem too bad at first and it wasn't very far to travel at all, especially after the lengthily travel time that we had become accustomed to in London. We were convinced she would settle in quickly as her pleasant nature made her easy to get along with and she had always attracted friends similar in nature to her. My favourite quality in Lorah-Kelly was that she always seemed so happy and carefree! She took delight in so much, complained about so little and expressed gratitude whenever she could. She truly was a blessing to all who knew her, which is why you can imagine why her depression came as a shock to us!

We had been so busy adjusting to this new life ourselves that we barely noticed Lorah-Kelly's change in demeanour. The change was subtle and to all intents and purposes, she seemed content at home. Perhaps the fact that she was quiet by nature meant that we missed the turmoil that was going on inside of her. Occasionally she mentioned that she was having trouble making friends at school and at the time I thought this very odd, as she had always found it easy to make friends. My advice to her was to give it a bit of time and not to lose heart.

A little more time passed and she revealed that it wasn't that she couldn't make friends but the problem was that she didn't like anyone that she had made friends with. After some investigation, we discovered that she was unable to find anyone that shared her values and morals. Simply put – she didn't fit in! It was only years later, when she shared her testimony in church, that we realised the depth of her struggle during this time. However, it is not the struggle I want to focus on, it is what she did with her struggle that is so important.

It was another beautiful summer's morning and we were stuck in a queue of traffic. Being stuck in traffic yet again with Lorah-Kelly and Jordan in the car, was actually quite pleasant! This was one of the few opportunities we had for some really good girly chats. I loved driving the girls to school, listening to 'their' music and hearing their thoughts and opinions on all sorts of things. On this particular morning, during one of our usual chats, Lorah-Kelly said something that would change the rest of our lives! She had made a decision, a very profound decision, and she shared it with Jordan and I as we waited for the traffic to ebb forward. Little did we know that crisp summer's morning how much this decision would change EVERYTHING for our family and many others too. This is what she said,

"Mommy, I am not going to go to school anymore to find friends like me. My school is going to become my mission field and I am going to win my friends to Jesus. That is the only way I am going to have friends like me!"

Her decision was made and she declared it to us. It seemed simple enough and I was very proud of her for finding a positive angle in her time of struggle. Little did we know that on that fine summer's morning, stuck in the traffic in our little red car, that Lorah-Kelly had moved the rudder and turned the compass of our entire family's life in a completely different direction. Her 'little' decision, made from her place of struggle, would affect thousands of lives for all of eternity.

Time passed and Lorah-Kelly, true to her word, began to see her friends through different eyes. They were no longer there to please her but she was there to reach out to them. It wasn't long before Lorah-Kelly's vision started to grow which meant she needed to recruit helpers! And so we had another little life changing conversation on another day in the car on the way to school. She said,

"Mommy, do you remember when you used to run a youth group in South Africa for all those children?"

"Yes" I said suspiciously

"Do you think we could do something like that again?"

"Of course" I said quite relieved.

Youth groups were the one thing I was confident in, as I had worked with children for several years back in South Africa. I had forgotten that the groups I had worked with had been with children at the same age as my children, when they were much younger. Now my children were teenagers. This was a completely new ball game to me, but that penny would sink in a little later on, when it was too late to back out!

And so it was agreed that we would start off with a girl's night at our home where Lorah-Kelly would invite over some of her new girl friends from school. It was around this time that the latest addition to our family had arrived, our baby boy, Daniel. We were sure we would manage though, it wasn't like we were doing anything big, and so we just got on with it. It was such a fun night with five teenage girls, just hanging out, chatting, eating pizza and playing silly games. I had as much fun as they did.

It wasn't long before the girls wanted to invite some boys to join in on our Friday night fun, and so our girl's night expanded into a guys and girls night. We continued to meet every Friday and the group of teenagers continued to grow. At this point Eric was roped in as many of the young boys were interested in playing guitar and they heard of Eric's amazing musical abilities. The group continued to grow and we became good friends with about twenty teenagers. Talking about God wasn't officially on the agenda, we just had fun together, but the teenagers quickly realised that we were Christians when we chatted about church openly when the subject came up.

It was time. We had to tell them. We were growing very fond of this group of awesome teenagers and to hide the truth from them would be wrong, very wrong. We had to tell them about Jesus. How could we love those kids so much and leave them hell bound? So we told them! I prepared a slide show on Power Point where I used the C.S Lewis story of Narnia to share the gospel message with the children. It had just come out on the cinema and so seemed a relevant angle to use. At the end of the presentation, I gave them an opportunity to accept Jesus as their Lord and Saviour and eight of the teenagers responded positively. It was such a beautiful moment, such an incredible privilege to lead these precious teenagers in a prayer that would change their lives forever.

Friday nights had turned a corner and things would never be the same again. We continued to have fun but now we also had baby Christians to feed and so we added more structure to the evening. Slowly but surely we incorporated a little bit of Biblical teaching to our fun and games and when the teenagers needed a good heart to heart we would often offer to pray with them too.

At this time, we were attending a church that was one hour's drive away from our home. After moving to Cheltenham, we had visited several local churches and didn't feel at home anywhere. We discovered this lovely church on our way back from a holiday in Wales one summer, and it instantly felt like home to us. An hour's drive to get to this church that we loved so much was accepted as we started attending every Sunday. This did however mean that we were unable to take all the new Christians to church with us each week and the only spiritual food they got was what we fed them on Friday nights.

Friday night's group continued to grow and teenagers continued to be saved. Our program went from a casual fun and games night to a structured youth program and it wasn't long before we were training up teams and leaders to help us make the evening a success. When the group became too big for our home we rented a venue close to Lorah-Kelly's school so that even more people could join in. Friday nights became really big. We would arrive an hour before the advertised starting time to set up a full band, sound desk and lighting scaffolding. Our teams consisted of:

1. **Welcome Team** whose role was to meet and greet people and to serve coffee,

2. **Production Team** whose role was to handle all the gear, setup, sound and lighting,

3. **IT Team** whose role was to manage the computer and projector for the song words on the big screen, along with Power Point games and a DVD Bible presentation,

4. **Band** who played a mixed set of secular and worship songs each Friday,

5. **Events Team** who organised special events, trips, shows and dance items,

6. **Media Team** whose role was to video record the news for each week, which was also projected onto the big screen.

It was at this point that we realised that these young people needed more discipleship than we were giving them on a Friday night. We made an appointment with our pastor to discuss this matter. Our plan was to run a discipleship group for those who were already saved, on a Sunday when we arrived home from our church in Wales. This would leave us free to focus on the unsaved on Fridays and to continue with fun and games for all.

Eric, Lorah-Kelly, Jordan, Dave (who I will tell you about a bit later on) and I went to a meeting with our pastor to ask his permission to start a Sunday discipleship group for our new Christians. We left this meeting with permission to plant a church! Looking back, we still don't know what happened. A CHURCH! What? How? Questions plagued us but the challenge excited us and so we all said, "OK God, if you want us to plant a church then so be it!"

Chapter 2
Never Cancel

Never Cancel

2006 → **2007** →

"God, we are not growing, shall we close this group down?" This was the question we were asking God in the same year that we started the Friday night youth group. Earlier that year we had started a connect group in our home on Thursday evenings. This group however was not producing the same results that the Friday night group was. Connect groups were exactly that, small groups of people from church getting together during the week to connect with each other. Bible study was not the focus on these evenings but building deep and meaningful relationships was. We enjoyed a meal together, chatted and laughed together and then closed with a time of prayer. Our hope was that when we invited people who weren't Christians that they would feel comfortable and have fun too. Many times Christians try to invite people who aren't Christians to Bible study groups, which don't always work out too well. Perhaps in the past it may have worked but in England in 2007 this was not a good strategy, which is why the connect group approach was adopted.

Eric and I had always loved going to a connect group in London and in our new church in Wales, so we volunteered to start one at our home as soon as the church asked for connect group hosts. We laboured in prayer for our neighbours, baked them cookies and did whatever kind deeds we could to win their favour but not one of them ever accepted our invitation to come to our connect group. Getting to know the parents of the youth group children proved difficult too and they also never came to our connect group. From time to time we had a couple from our previous connect group join us on Thursdays and occasionally one of the mothers of Jordan's friend from school came along too. Dave, however, came every single Thursday without fail!

Dave was from our church in Wales. He lived even further north than we did and so it made perfect sense that he should join our connect group rather than travel an hour and a half to meet up with people. Some Thursdays we would have a lovely time with five or six of us and other Thursdays it would just be Eric, Dave and I. After about six months, we began to question whether God was with us and why we were not growing. Dave continued to join us every Thursday even though it was just the three of us.

Eric and I had made a firm commitment to each other shortly after starting the connect group, saying that no matter who turned up or who didn't turn up, we would NEVER cancel connect group. True to our word, we never did. In the end it was only Eric, Dave and I every Thursday but we never cancelled. We continued to meet with Dave, we ate together, prayed together and got to know each other really, really well.

Soon Dave started joining us on a Friday night too and helped us with our youth group as he had many years of experience in this area. It wasn't long before we realised what a treasure Dave was. He was the most amazing person we had ever known. There was nothing that was too much trouble for him and despite his own personal struggles at the time, he always seemed so positive. Knowing Dave was such a joy and our friendship grew from strength to strength.

Thursdays almost seemed like Dave night and not connect group, which is why we questioned what God was doing. Connect groups are supposed to grow and then multiply into two connect groups and then grow and multiply again. Our group was not growing at all so we asked God if we should close it down and focus on doing things that would bear more fruit. God's answer seemed to be 'no'! Eric and I did not have peace about stopping our meetings on Thursdays and so we continued to meet and we continued to invite people in the hope that our group would grow. It never did grow.

And we never cancelled. Dave, Eric and I continued to connect week after week.

Yes, there are times when things that don't bear fruit should be closed and yes there are seasons for everything. But if I were to write here in this book a rule or a step that you should take when planting a church then I would fail you. You see, you can't replace being lead by the Holy Spirit! There is no recipe for building a church and there is no growth formula for Christian gatherings. For our connect group, for that season of our life, we knew not to close it, there was no logical reason, in fact it didn't seem logical at all, but we never cancelled.

Little did we know how important this special bond between the three of us would be! I can't imagine how things would have turned out if we didn't cultivate a deep and meaningful relationship with our friend Dave. 'Never cancel' became one of our guidelines, if we were in doubt and didn't know which way to turn, we simply agreed to not cancel. It's not a rule, which would be as silly as the Pharisees were when they made six hundred and thirteen rules out of the Ten Commandments! We don't make rules but we do have little catch phrases that help us when we are not sure and God won't say anything either way. If it were a rule then we couldn't have cancelled that one night when we really needed a rest or on the other occasion after Amy was born. We would have been a slave to our own rules and this is not God's way, is it? His only "rule" is to love God and to love people. We say we never cancel because otherwise every time we were in doubt or had an attack of laziness or tiredness we would probably cancel!

Saying that we never cancel helped us to push through when we were tired and helped us to pitch up when we didn't want to. It got us through dry seasons and it helped us stay focused. Again, it all boils down to trusting the Holy Spirit. We say never cancel because we are prone to laziness as human beings; this is our safeguard to make sure we keep going. There are no rules; there simply cannot be rules when building a church, if God didn't give them, then neither should we.

Chapter 3
Do Not Grow Weary

Do Not Grow Weary

2006 → 2007 → **2008** →

"He made it!" That was the remark I made to Eric when I read Ewen's very first blog post. His post was rich with love for Jesus and gratitude for what He had done in his life. My heart swelled with pride.

Ewen was turning eighteen and I felt as much pride for him as I did for my own children.

I first met Ewen when he was fifteen years old in 2008. He dropped in to see what was happening at our Friday night youth group when we were meeting in the community centre. Clearly he was a trouble maker. That night, I also noticed a display of deep cuts all over his arms. The image is still vividly imprinted in my mind as I knew that those bleeding wounds on his arms represented the state of his heart.

Many teenagers came to us with heart wrenching stories full of hurt and confusion. The first time I met Ewen, his manner and body language made a clear statement that he was not to be messed with. His foul language and rough exterior combined with the cigarettes, drugs and alcohol defined him. Worst of all I could see that he really believed that this was his true self. After a few incidents at youth I began to dread his return, it was clear he was there to make trouble and assert himself as a ruffian.

The first time I caught a glimmer of hope was when I ran a session on identity and Ewen surprisingly participated. I spoke of the confusion that I saw the young people dealing with and delved into the fact that they didn't really know who they were. As I spoke I saw Ewen's eyes well up. He nodded continuously as I described what I saw in the lives of young people and then he spoke of his inner turmoil. I had to hold back my tears. Behind his rough exterior was a heart of gold suppressed by anger and confusion.

That day changed my life, I began to pray for him and begged God for his salvation. It seemed impossible that someone so rough would soften enough to allow God in but when I prayed I placed the picture of his teary eyes in the forefront of my mind. On the 21st September 2008 God answered my prayer. It was our very first church service and Ewen was our very first salvation, our precious first fruit. Even now as I remember that special day I am overwhelmed by God's goodness and mercy.

Since then God has done amazing things in Ewen's life, too much to begin to write here. At school the teachers wrote him off. Almost daily he was in some sort of trouble and his grades were so bad that they didn't expect him to finish school. It wasn't long before the teachers were gobsmacked by the change in Ewen and more than that they were shocked by his improved grades. I guess you could imagine their reaction when he announced his plans to go to university! What the teachers had written off, God had declared a *'future and a hope*[2]*'* to. Ewen has since achieved the grades he needed to get into the school he wanted. No teachers' words define him now. The word of God is the *'light to his path*[3]*'*. Ewen knows who he is and that he is called to do significant damage to the darkness that nearly killed him. His testimony is powerful and his influence in this nation will be too.

Yes, God did change Ewen's life, but more than that, Ewen has changed mine. I love him as my own son and am a very proud mama. To add a cherry to the top of the cake, Ewen wrote the most beautiful song[1] on our debut album[2] which I had the honour of singing with Lorah-Kelly. It's a powerful song written by a truly grateful heart.

---

[1] I Know by Ewen Bowen
[2] King's Square by D7 Band

And let us not grow weary while doing good, for in due season we shall reap if we do not lose heart.

- *Galatians 6:9*

But as for you, brethren, do not grow weary in doing good.

- *2 Thessalonians 3:13*

That day, his eighteenth birthday, was one of those special days, the day where I reaped a rich reward. I confess I did grow weary; perhaps I did lose heart a bit too. There were many sleepless nights praying Ewen through rough patches during college. At times I wanted to give up but I couldn't, there was always that *'what if?'* What if he was only one day away from victory? What if he really needed our love and support for just a little longer to make it? What if something really bad happened to him because we lost heart? What if he was intended to be the prime minister of England and we let him slip away? The 'what ifs' lined up and suddenly the small sacrifice of prayer didn't seem such a big deal after all. So we prayed, we loved him and every now and then we had a few awkward chats too.

The reward for me that day was to see him celebrate his eighteenth birthday knowing deep down inside of my heart that he had made it. He is safe. He pulled through the dark times and I am utterly convinced that he is going to be all that God wants him to be! I don't think the verses about growing weary meant that we should not grow weary. Growing weary will happen. If we are working hard, there is no escaping weariness. No, for me, the not growing weary is of 'doing good'. You will get tired but don't stop. Don't stop doing good even though you are tired. Keep doing good despite the weariness. Here are some tips for dealing with the weariness that will come from time to time:

Have Rest

Holidays, weekends away, random nights off, lie ins, etc. These are all essential ingredients to surviving ministry. If you don't plan these rests they won't happen and if you don't commit to them they won't happen. Where possible, actually set your holidays in your church calendar at the beginning of the year, this gives you something to look forward to during the year.

Plan weekends away too and when necessary take a spontaneous break here and there. Most importantly, don't feel guilty about sleeping late or napping when you need to. Most pastors do not work a strict nine to five job, we work at night and we work weekends and we could pretty much be working all the time. Occasionally if we have a meeting in the evening we will sleep a little late that same morning, especially if we had a late night the night before too. I am not talking about sleeping the day away or waking up at lunch time. Perhaps wake up an hour or two later than usual, it is amazing how much difference that can make to your day.

Eric would often take short ten to twenty minute naps in the afternoon when we first started church. He was running all day and all night as he was teaching music to earn a living and running the church. His energy levels were quite low then too but a short power nap in the afternoon was all he needed to get him through a full evening of work.

Have Fun

What is the point to life if we are not enjoying it? I would hate to see my children work very hard for me all the time and never smile or laugh or enjoy their lives. I would not feel good about it at all and would prefer them not to work for me than lack fun in their lives. As a mother, one of my biggest pleasures in life is my children's pleasure. When they are thrilled I am thrilled, when they are blessed I am blessed, when they are happy I am happy and when they are having fun I am smiling. The opposite is true too, when my children are sad I am concerned, when they are stressed I am unhappy, when they are overworking I am not pleased.

God is a father too and it is no different for Him. He takes pleasure in our pleasure and cannot be pleased when we over work, especially if we are overworking in His name. Just look at the story of Mary and Martha, which women pleased Jesus most? Mary pleased Jesus, the one who wasn't stressed with over work but was happily sitting at Jesus' feet, hanging out with Him and catching up on all the latest news from Jesus' travels.

Eric and I have a weekly date night which is the highlight of our week. We also have a weekly family day every Saturday where we all spend time together. I absolutely love these special moments that we have each week. No matter what has happened during the week, no matter how tired we are, date night and family day always happen and they always refresh us.

Parties, celebrations, dinners out, sailing, mountain boarding, you name it; whatever is fun for you, do it. Don't put it off; don't stop living just because you are serving God. I can assure you it does not please God. When you smile and are experiencing the thrill of this wonderful life that God has given us, He smiles too. So you can't lose, not only will you have more fun but you will be pleasing God more too.

Have Friends

You would think that this is an obvious one but it's not. Too often we get so busy, so caught up with caring for people and building the church that we neglect our own friendships. One thing I noticed with church planting is that friendships change. People who were once friends stop understanding you. Unless they have been there and done that it is very difficult for them to understand. Planting a church is not what it seems and few will understand, even though some may be willing to try.

We learned that we needed to understand that different relationships had different purposes. Most of the people in church look to us as leaders and they cannot be our friends. They could not handle a friendship with us and we must respect those boundaries. Leading them and serving them is our function and we cannot expect anything back from them. You might disagree with me on this one but I have found this to be true for me.

Other friends are on the team with us, they understand us better because they are in the front line with us, we can relax a little more around them and have a friendship with them but we still should not confide in most of them. They too cannot handle it and it would put an unnecessary burden on them. There is nothing that can change that and so we must respect those boundaries. They are not responsible to make the leadership decisions that we are, they do not carry the weight that we do and although they are our friends, they are still looking to us for leadership and so we should not neglect leading them.

Eric and I do have Dave on our pastoral team; we share a special bond with him as he has been a pastor previously, he has been on this journey with us for long enough and we know that he totally gets 'it'. Dave has seen us on our good, bad and ugly days, he knows the pressures we face and when we do slip up he is the one to cover us. Everyone should have a Dave in their life!

After discovering this harsh reality in the area of friends we asked God to give us friends that were pastors too. We asked God for people that would totally understand our position and not need our leadership. Our desire was to learn from them, share what we had learned but all on a mutual level of friendship.

These sorts of friendships are essential when planting a church. God provided such wonderful friends to us, friends that have been or still are pastors. It was incredible to see what else God did with our friendships. Not only did we have wonderful friends but our churches became friends. We loved and served each other, we had occasional combined events, we served where they had lack and they served where our church had lack. The synergy was fantastic and may God bring you and I more friends like these.

Understanding the need for friends and the different level of friendships is crucial in church planting. Everything we do is relational but understanding the purpose of each relationship is very important.

Know God

Now you must think I am nuts - of course you must know God if you are planting a church! Well let me tell you, it is easy to lose sight of God when you are too busy. What was once an hour or two of passionate prayer and connection with God can quickly become a rushed five minutes in the morning before you go out and tend to your/His business. What was once a love and passion for the Bible can quickly become a chore to throw yet another sermon together. What was once an entire evening of personal time with God, a moment of being with Him and loving Him can quickly be lost due to lack of free evenings.

King David once prayed, *"Restore to me the joy of Your salvation, and uphold me by Your generous Spirit."*[4] I never understood that very well until I got busy with leading our church. I lost touch with God. My relationship with Him was not what it used to be and when I realised what had happened I was grieved by it. I questioned how I could be ministering to people and leading people and yet be so disconnected from God. I was still saying the same things, my words were still 'correct' but my heart was cold. I did love God and I knew He would *never leave me or forsake me*[5] but somehow my passion for Him became dull and my salvation was familiar.

When I realised this, I repented for being so familiar with the cross and asked God to restore to me the joy of my salvation as King David had once prayed. It never occurred to me that I could never tell people about what Jesus did on the cross without being totally bowled over by it myself each and every time I spoke. It never occurred to me that it was possible to have a good 'sales pitch' for God but not be living what I was 'selling'.

I got on my knees and begged God for forgiveness; I did not want to do this without Him. I know many pastors can maintain a church without a true relationship with God, I know it exists but I did not want to be like that. It was then that I began to set aside special time to spend with Jesus again, like I used to before I got busy. I lingered in His presence for hours and refused to be interrupted by anyone or even my own thoughts.

I would love to say that the fire was instantly rekindled but it wasn't. I struggled to connect with God, I didn't feel the same things I used to, I wasn't even sure if He was with me. Well that's what it felt like anyway, of course He was with me, but perhaps I was the one that wasn't fully present. It was hard to focus, my mind would wonder, my to do list would shout at me, my thoughts would dance around in my head. Of course God was with me but I was the one that couldn't find the stillness that was needed to know Him like I once did.

A quick fix was not what I was looking for and so I began to set aside regular time to spend with God. It is a relationship after all and if you don't invest in it, it will grow cold. Marriages don't survive without investments, teenagers don't connect well with their parents without investment and so neither does your relationship with God. He misses us when we don't spend time with Him and He is jealous[6] when we love other things more than Him.

It was God who said, *"Be still, and know that I am God"*[7]. Perhaps He knew how our minds would race around and how busyness would creep in between Him and us. Perhaps we cannot truly know our God intimately if we don't take the time to be still, and know Him. You can build a church without an intimate relationship with God but why would you want to? It's like saying you can build a marriage without an intimate relationship with your spouse, but why would you want to? It's the intimacy that makes the relationship, it's the intimacy that is most fun and it is the intimacy that bears fruit!

Prioritise intimacy with God, don't let church work get in the way of knowing God. Grow in love with Him, stay intimate with Him, keep close to Him and see how your church will flourish and bear much fruit as a result!

Chapter 4
A Wolf and Abandonment

A Wolf and

Abandonment

2006 → 2007 → 2008 → 2009 →

℘ It was 2am and we were still sitting in our living room chatting with the two young men that might well have been our future sons-in-law. Perhaps that was looking too far ahead, but as a mother, I was always on the lookout for potential husbands for my girls. Very 'Pride and Prejudice' I know, but unless you are a mother with young ladies at home, you will never understand the insane drive within a mother to find a suitable match for her girls.

Lorah-Kelly, Jordan, Eric and I sat with the boys and were glad that we had finally met some Christians that seemed to be mature in their faith. Up until this point, we had struggled along with raising the lost and the baby Christians that were born in our church. Determined not to build a church on transfer growth, we pushed forward with what and whom we had. It was a relief though, to think that perhaps God was sending some labourers to us, to help us with our work.

We began spending more and more time with these two young boys and were quite sure that they were sent as helpers to help us stir up our young teenage believers. Very quickly we began to bond and it wasn't long before they started bringing their friends and family to church. We were thrilled, not only were they mature Christians but they were also bringers.

At the same time we started relying heavily on another family that joined us as soon as the church was launched. They too had been Christians for some time and they were also bringing their friends and family to church. We were growing steadily and everything looked great. For the sake of privacy we will change everyone's names in this chapter, let's call the two young boys Matt and Sam and the family the Smiths.

We also discovered that Matt and Sam, along with their friends and family, were well acquainted with the Smiths too. It all seemed good, everyone knew everyone and they were all getting along very well. Everything seemed fine and dandy, people were getting saved almost every Sunday and church was growing steadily each week. We trusted Matt and Sam with our daughters and allowed them to go out together to socialise. Great friendships were forming and there was nothing to be concerned about, or so we thought.

It wasn't long before we allowed the Smiths to host a connect group and to lead in our church. They truly were a wonderful family and they had been with us from the beginning, so it made sense to allow them to grow into a leadership role.

Matt and Sam started meeting up with our young Christians for Bible study so that they could help them find their way. We didn't offer the sort of 'thing' they were doing 'officially' in our church but we figured that there would be no harm in a bunch of young people getting together to study the Bible and pray for each other. It was quite nice actually; it took the pressure off of us to keep finding new and creative ways to 'feed' our young people.

After some time we noticed that the young Christians were not doing so well. We could not put a finger on it but the fruit simply didn't seem good. A few weeks later, we started to feel concerned - we were alerted to the fact that the Smith's were hosting a Bible study in their home for all our young teenage Christians. Again, probably not something that should raise an alarm, but we were concerned because it was being led by Matt and Sam's father. Their father was not a member of our church and had openly come against Eric and I as leaders, as well as against the pastor who had released us to plant our church.

We called the Smith's in for a meeting and lovingly explained our concerns and that as leaders in our church; they really shouldn't start things up without at least chatting to us about it first. The content of the Bible studies were discussed which raised further concerns as it turned out that they were being taught exclusively about the end times and the Book of Revelation - not a subject that we would jump into with new Christians.

The Smith's received what we had to say very well and agreed with our concerns. According to their own free will they stopped the Bible study at their home as they realised that it was doing more damage than good. This of course infuriated Matt and Sam's father as he could not understand why they felt that they had to do this. He continued to visit the Smith's home almost daily to try and 'teach' them about the Bible and the error of their ways with regards to rejecting his Bible study. He also made it very clear that Eric and I were not fit to lead a church. A few weeks passed and we discovered that the new Christians were confused about many things. They came to us with questions but sadly some of them went back to Matt and Sam's father for guidance.

It wasn't long before Matt and Sam became upset with our rejection of their father. After many long debates in person and very long emails with them, they left our church. They stayed in touch with our daughters and most of the teenagers and then began stirring the teenagers up against us. Soon the teenagers started leaving our church too. Many of them were totally confused and had lost the way of their simple faith. They had too many unanswered questions. Questions that really didn't need answers but the teaching they received blinded them to the simple love of Jesus and opened up a theological can of worms – something they were not ready to deal with.

Eric and I were grieved.

Months later, the Smiths, and all their immediate and distant family, and their friends, left our church too. They too became confused and found it difficult to find their way forward in our church. A chain reaction had started and anyone linked to the chain ended up leaving. We went from what we thought was a thriving, flourishing church to a struggling church with few left in attendance. We had lost at least sixty percent of our congregation. Sadly, most of them didn't even go on to join another church, they simply went back to worldly things.

During this season, we took a great deal of counsel from our pastor. He very wisely advised us of every step we should take and we followed his advice to the letter. In fact, in one meeting Eric actually wrote down every word he said and regurgitated it word for work to a couple that we were told to discipline.

Our mother church encouraged us every step of the way and gave us all the support they could, which is why it was a real shock when they too cut ties with us. Three weeks notice was all we were given to set up a new church and take over all the bills. If ever we felt totally confused and alone it was during the November of 2009. It was the end of a very difficult year, we had worked hard, seen many saved but lost too many people when the 'wolf' attacked. We were still wounded and recovering from this horrible process when the bomb of abandonment hit us. Our mother church was not happy with our numbers. In a nutshell, we had not grown sufficiently and were not producing enough income to sustain us. They wanted to pull the plug on the church.

Shocked and horrified, we considered the way forward. We were given a choice, either we closed the church down completely or we went back to being a connect group and found a way to transport everyone to our mother church each Sunday. The third option was to continue on our own. Our pastor said he would release us with his blessing and no hard feelings.

Tom

As we contemplated the huge decision we had to make we were plagued by the faces of all the people in our church that had come to know Jesus. One face in particular stood out, an ex-heroin addict, Tom, who had come such a long way. I remember the day I met Tom. His sheer size was enough to make a lasting impression on me; he is a very tall man. To be honest he did frighten me at first. He was wearing a black, full length coat and had a dark look about him. Sweat dotted his forehead and his eyes were dull with a much glazed look about them. Slurred speech combined with regular spitting left me praying that saliva didn't land near my mouth and infect me with some sort of disease. I introduced myself to Tom and offered him a sandwich and a cup of coffee, only half a cup of course as he would have spilled it all over himself.

I didn't mean this in an insulting way at all, it was just that I had learned to recognise that the shaky hands of a drug addict caused them to spill hot coffee all over the place. I had learned this the hard way, by spending my Sunday mornings wiping up trails of coffee spills all the way from the coffee lounge, down the steps, across the landing, down some more steps and out to the front door of the building. All these things make up the reality of inviting street people into our church.

How did Tom find his way to a church - through a simple offer of a free sandwich. One of our team found him huddled on the side of the street suffering from heroine withdrawals. He was shivering partly from the cold and partly from the horrible effects of the drug that had consumed his life. Most of the words said to him that morning were a blur I'm sure, but thankfully he did hear the word sandwich. He was being offered free sandwiches which led him to our church.

After a few weeks of Tom coming to church he confessed that he felt like a hypocrite. Eric assured him that he was very welcome to only come for the sandwich - no strings attached. He then went on to invite him to join us for the church service if he ever wanted to join us. Tom sensed Eric's sincerity and felt comfortable to stay for the church service. Since that day we have seen God do the most amazing things in Tom's life. He surrendered his life to Jesus, came off drugs and alcohol, got a home and begun the process of rebuilding his life. Eleven weeks after he first walked through the church doors we had the privilege of dedicating his son to God. It is incredible to see how God has restored Tom's relationship with his son and radically changed this little boy's life.

The thought of telling Tom that church would close down was unbearable. It would be too complicated to explain how things work and too much information for such a young Christian who saw church as a 'good' place to be. Tom's face stayed in our minds as we weighed up our options. Another face popped up, a really strange but lovely alcoholic who at times came to church totally drunk, but who always danced and sang in the worship with so much passion and sincerity. We never really understood this man but when he worshipped we knew his love for Jesus was real. He hadn't yet found freedom in several areas but the thought of telling him that church would be no more was simply unacceptable. Actually, I couldn't see any other church allowing this sort of behaviour during a service, we were quite an unusual church after all. The faces continued to flash before us and we realised that there was no way we could just ditch them and go back to being a connect group – they had grown to love our church and so had we and there was something special about church which we would lose if we only had a connect group.

The option of transporting people to the mother church was no option at all, there were too many people, it was an hour's drive away, and that simply wouldn't work at all. We discussed it with Dave and Lorah-Kelly and the team, prayed about it and decided to keep going no matter what that meant. It was unanimous; no one wanted to stop the work that we had started. We warned the team of the hard work that was ahead and the incredible sacrifice that would be required. This didn't deter them one bit, closing church was simply not even thinkable. Encouraged by their determination, we made our decision known to our pastor.

He said he understood and released us with his blessing, saying that he was still always there for us if we needed him for anything at all. He also said that he would support us in any way that he could and he wished us well. Again, you can imagine our surprise when the man that handled the church finances and the associate pastor announced that we had until the end of November to put everything in order.

It was the end of the first week in November, or there about. I contacted them and asked for mercy, asking if we could please have until the end of December so that we could have a clean start from 1st January 2010. We needed time to figure things out, this was such a shock and it would have been nice to have a period of transition or something.   Nevertheless, no mercy was given and three weeks was all we had.

Abandoned, alone, confused and completely unsure of anything at all was how we felt.   We questioned whether God had truly called us, we wondered if we had done something terribly wrong and most of all we wondered if we were up to the task ahead. Yet another deep end that we were thrown into and it was 'sink or swim' time.   Thankfully we had a fantastic team that were on this journey with us and they had no doubts that we would be fine.   And so on 1st December 2009 D7 Church was born!

Chapter 5
The Least and the Small

The Least and
the Small

2006 ▸ 2007 ▸ 2008 ▸ 2009 ▸ **2010** ▸

Lorah-Kelly brought a word to our pastors meeting one morning, a simple word but one that would change our perspective as a church. She started by reading a verse from the book of Isaiah.

"...the least of you will become a thousand, the smallest a mighty nation. I am the Lord, in its time I will do this swiftly."

- *Isaiah 60:22*

The Least of You

This could be talking about a small amount of people and could also mean the least of you as in Matthew 25:40 'Assuredly, I say to you, inasmuch as you did it to one of the least of these My brethren, you did it to Me.' At the time we were least in every possible way. Our attendance numbers were very low and at the same time we were reaching out intensively to homeless people and welcoming them into our church.

The Smallest

This could be talking about a small amount of people or literally the smallest or youngest children. Again, we were smallest in both senses of the word as we were small in numbers and the kids team were doing an excellent job in raising our little ones in kids' church. Lorah-Kelly then went on to share another verse that has defined us. "The Spirit of the Lord is on me, because he has anointed me to proclaim good news to the poor. He has sent me to proclaim freedom for the prisoners   and recovery of sight for the blind, to set the oppressed free, to proclaim the year of the Lord's favour."

- *Luke 4:18-19*

The Blind and Prisoners

This is perhaps not literally blind or actual prisoners but those in bondage who need freedom. Later on that year, about six months after Lorah-Kelly shared this simple word with us, we could see how God was bringing it to pass. We did take some direction from these verses and did what we could to serve 'the least and the small' in our community.   We made sure that we always considered the street people and made them feel welcome in our church services. On a practical level we invited them into the foyer before church, served them the best coffee possible, the nicest sandwiches and some scrumptious muffins.

From time to time people questioned our approach saying that we were silly to be spending so much money on these things, but we knew that it was vital that we served 'the least' as we would serve Jesus himself. Jesus did say that if we did it to one of the least of these we did it to Him.

We also touched them. This may sound like a silly thing to add but I can't stress enough the importance of physical touch when loving people. Eric and I made a point, whenever we greeted someone in our church, to look them in the eye and to touch them in some way with a loving physical touch. This often meant hugging a smelly drunk from the street or shaking hands with someone that had clearly not washed their hands in weeks. Yes, it was difficult at first but we simply accepted it as something valuable that we did for the least. It was easy if you saw it as doing it to Jesus - we were hugging Jesus and we were shaking Jesus' hand.

On a practical note, we did have hand sanitiser available on the table where we served food and I often sanitised my hands before picking up some food to eat. Also, when we have newborn babies in church, some mothers allowed the street people to hold them if they asked, but we did politely ask them to sanitise their hands first ,as the little ones had not yet built up their immune systems. I taught the mothers that they should never feel that they have to do this, it wouldn't be wrong to say no to someone who wanted to hold their baby. However, if they didn't mind, it would be sensible to take obvious precautions. We eliminate the feeling of 'them and us' but making sure that everything was applicable to everyone. I too sanitised my hands before picking up a newborn baby. It's sensible to do so if you think about it.

And so we continued to ask God to grow our love for the least and the small. In time we began to realise that no matter what a person looked like or smelled like on the outside, they all had a fascinating story to tell. We learned to take time to listen to each new person's story, to get to really know them and to love them as a precious person created by God.

Loving the small was wonderful! Little children often set the tone in our church with their innocent but truthful comments or their sincere heartfelt worship. We made the children an important part of church life and took educating them in God's ways seriously. Kids Zone was not a babysitting club so that the parents could enjoy the service. Kids Zone was a place where the gospel was shared, where the little ones learned about Jesus and how to pray, how to give their tithe and how to trust God. Children were born again in Kids Zone and filled with the Holy Spirit. Dave, who led this team, loved each child and understood the privilege and pressure of being a Youth Pastor.

One thing that we realised was that many of the sad stories we heard from people started before they turned ten years old. They were either raped, abused, witnessed a crime or had some sort of trauma before they turned ten years old. If the devil was pitching this young we needed to reach out to the little ones under ten years old too! It made more sense to focus on teaching little ones about Jesus than it did spending hours and hours counselling messed up adults!

Chapter 6
Pitch up & Press On

Pitch Up and
Press On

There have been days when I have wanted to give up. MANY DAYS! Tiredness had overcome me and I had grown weary. It's not the sort of weariness that can be solved by sleep. This sort of weariness was deep down within my soul; it seemed to seep right down into my bones and made my belly ache. I had known many of these sorts of days.

There had also been many Sundays when I had not wanted to go to church. Yes, I confess, many Sundays when I had just wanted to stay in bed and leave Eric to get on with it. A few Sundays I managed to make it into the car and all the way to church but then had just stayed in the car outside church and cried. On a few occasions I had even started the car and reversed out of the parking space with the intention of driving away. Despite the battles that have raged within my soul some Sundays, I have always pitched up. Not always with the best attitude, not always with the enthusiasm that I should have, but I pitched up. That is step one to surviving the rough seasons!

Let me describe how bad it got at one point! During the week Eric was telling me that it was his desire that I enjoyed the journey. I had been particularly down in the dumps and very negative about everything. I loved God with all my heart but was drained by church. During a conversation one evening I told Eric how much I hated church and began to spew all my complaints over him,

"I don't even know if God is with us, surely if He were with us there would be more fruit and at least some growth? It has been two years now and people have come and gone but our weekly attendance is still the same as when we started! In fact it has dropped!

Surely if God were with us things would have been showing some improvement by now? How about signs and wonders? We are supposed to be seeing the mighty hand of God move but all we see is hard work day in and day out with no fruit!

Do the people that we are working so hard for even love God? Do they read their Bible and pray or do they only love the benefits of church? They come for the free food and all the nice things we do for them, but do they come because they love God?

Even our team! I am not convinced that they have a deep relationship with God, they just enjoy the cool stuff about church, but do they love God? I am not convinced any more. I am not sure if any of this is worth

it! Those of us that have been doing this for two years are drained now; we have lost our passion and are working ourselves to death — for what? So that others can come in and sponge off of our work and give nothing back?

I am tired, I am fed up and I hate church on Sundays. I don't even want to go anymore. I dread Sundays and don't have the energy for all this."

And so the complaining and grumbling continued. I was weary and I wasn't convinced that God was even with us. I had lost my passion for the House of God and wanted out. Although I wanted out I would never leave or quit. Something inside of me had to keep going. There was always that one little 'what if?' *What if* breakthrough was around the corner? *What if* people really did love God and just needed more time? *What if* God was testing us and our perseverance? *What if* I was wrong and this was just how it is?

The 'what ifs' plagued my mind and kept me motivated to pitch up Sunday after Sunday until breakthrough came — and it did come. It came in the most unexpected way too. It was a regular Sunday morning and I was doing what I always do – I pitched up and I did my best to do my part. I was on autopilot getting busy with doing what I had to do. After sorting out the kids, chatting to visitors, pouring some coffee and listening to a homeless woman's woes, I sat down to 'enjoy' the service.

This was a Sunday when I had the opportunity to participate in the worship and not lead it. I sat in the front row with the children. We sang a few songs and then the children started to get rowdy. They started singing passionately and loudly – all you could hear were their voices. Sweet sounds of four year olds were rising up to heaven singing, "Bless Your Holy name, bless Your Holy name, bless Your Holy name, bless Your Holy name"

It was a beautiful sound and I was humbled by their worship. I agreed with them and said, "Yes Lord, bless Your Holy name, you are so worthy of the awesome praise of these little ones, I know how much this must bless You. Bless Your Holy name Lord!" It wasn't my worship, it was their worship, but I knew how much it must have blessed God, and I was pleased for God that

He was receiving such pure worship this morning. It made me feel ashamed of my pitiful worship. He was God Almighty and deserved so much more than I was giving Him. My heart was softened and ready to receive the Word that my wonderful husband was about to preach! Little did I know that his sermon would rock my selfish world and totally blow my mind! It changed me back into the passionate, lover of God's House that I used to be. Without further ado, let me share his sermon with you – over to Eric!

Words from Solomon - the richest man who ever lived

I denied myself nothing my eyes desired; I refused my heart no pleasure. My heart took delight in all my work, and this was the reward for all my labour. Yet when I surveyed all that my hands had done and what I had toiled to achieve, everything was meaningless, a chasing after the wind; nothing was gained under the sun. So I hated life, because the work that is done under the sun was grievous to me. All of it is meaningless, a chasing after the wind.

- *Ecclesiastes 2:10-11, 17*

I'm <u>frustrated</u>. Life is useless, all useless. You spend your life working but what do you have to show for it? The world stays just the same.

- *Ecclesiastes 1:2-4*

I'm <u>tired</u>. The sun still rises, and it still goes down, the wind blows, round and round and back again. Every river flows into the sea... [then] the water returns to where the rivers began and starts all over again. Everything leads to weariness – a weariness too great for words...

- *Ecclesiastes 1:5-8*

I'm <u>unfulfilled</u>. ...No matter how much we see, we're never satisfied. No matter how much we hear, we're not content. History merely repeats itself.

- *Ecclesiastes 1:8-9*

Words from Paul who lived a totally opposite life

Three times I was beaten with rods, once I was pelted with stones, three times I was shipwrecked, I spent a night and a day in the open sea, I have been constantly on the move. I have been in danger from rivers, in danger from bandits, in danger from my fellow Jews, in danger from Gentiles; in danger in the city, in danger in the country, in danger at sea; and in danger from false believers. I have laboured and toiled and have often gone without sleep; I have known hunger and thirst and have often gone without food; I have been cold and naked. Besides everything else, I face daily the pressure of my concern for all the churches.

-   *2 Corinthians 11:25-28*

Therefore we do not lose heart. Though outwardly we are wasting away, yet inwardly we are being renewed day by day. For our light and momentary troubles are achieving for us an eternal glory that far outweighs them all. So we fix our eyes not on what is seen, but on what is unseen. For what is seen is temporary, but what is unseen is eternal.

-   *2 Corinthians 4:16-18*

What is the unseen in this day and age? Consider our church, did you know that:

1. For some people church is the highlight of their week.
Greatness is not what great people say about you. Greatness is what ordinary people, who can benefit you nothing, say about you.

2. Church is their only hope.
There are people relocating just to join us, wanting to be part of an awesome team and a church with a big vision. People that came to Christ through our hard work are now reaping the benefits of a new life and our church is their only hope as they survive each week.

3. We are building an awesome church.
People want to give financially to our church because they have recognised our work and vision. We can't lose sight of it. If you can see it you can have it. Breakthrough might be just around the corner.

It was at this point that I was completely humbled. As Eric preached I was able to see our church through someone else's eyes. It was as if God was showing our church to me through the street people's eyes and through the young people eyes, through the eyes of the lost and hurting. For too long I had lost that perspective and had merely looked at our church as the hard work that it truly is. As Eric preached my passion was rekindled. His sermon reminded my why I first fell in love with church, the same church that Jesus loved so much that He died for her[8].

My heart ached with repentance as I realised how hard I had become. As my mind wondered off, away from the sermon, I pondered on these things, asked God for forgiveness and determined not to let myself get into that state ever again. As I sat daydreaming I heard Eric's voice fade back in again as he said, "So what should we do then? How can we respond to this?"

1. Keep on showing up.

At just the right time we will reap a harvest of blessing if we don't give up.

- *Galatians 6:9*

Half of the battle is showing up. History is not kind to people who go back. People who haven't realised going back is never better will always struggle to find a reason to keep going in the face to adversity. The millions who went back from the brink of Canaan did not write the next chapter of the Bible, but Joshua and Caleb did.

2. Expect great things to happen.

To expect is to believe something will happen. Put your faith to work, expect God to pitch up in a huge way. Expect the unexpected. 'I am the Lord, is anything too hard for Me?'

-    *Jeremiah 32:27*

3. Press on.

But I focus on this one thing: Forgetting the past and looking forward to what lies ahead, I press on to reach the end of the race and receive the heavenly prize for which God, through Christ Jesus, is calling us.

-    *Philippians 3:13-14*

4. Make a habit to look through the eyes of faith.

Now all glory to God, who is able, through his mighty

power at work within us, to accomplish infinitely more than we might ask or think.

-   *Ephesians 3:20*

5 - Watch out.

That you do not lose what you have worked for, but that you may be rewarded fully.

-   *2 John 1:8*

6. Persevere.

Because... blessed is the man who perseveres.

-   *James 1:12*

7. Don't get tired.

So let's not get tired of doing what is good. At just the right time we will reap a harvest of blessing if we don't give up.

-   *Galatians 6:9*

And so God had mercy on me once again and spoke to me so beautifully through my wonderful husband's message that day. Perspective is so important and losing it can be disastrous. Also, don't underestimate the devil; he is very skilled at causing blindness.

Thankfully, I have had an awesome team that has also pitched up with me every Sunday no matter what. For these guys I am truly grateful. I am sure they too have had their wrestles and struggles but you would never be able to tell. Our team has been our strength even when individually we have been weak and pathetic.

Chapter 7
Build a Great Team

Build a Great
Team

Church is not a one man or one woman job! It can't be mostly because God says *that no flesh should glory in His presence.*[9] If we could successfully build a flourishing church on our own then it is quite likely that we would become proud and even arrogant. God made us relational and dependant on each other in order to do His will. Eric and I realised this right from the start, we knew we could not pull it off on our own and so we got stuck into recruiting team members right from the word 'go'!

Before even thinking about planting a church, I would highly recommend building a team that will work with you and support you no matter what! It's not about quantity but about quality. A small team with the right heart will do so much more than a large team with a bad attitude. Sounds easy doesn't it, but I can assure you that finding people with a great heart that will just shut up and get on with it is not easy!

Our team started way back in 2006 without us even realising it. They were at our home weekly, doing life with us more than with their own parents. Little did we realise that all the seeds we were sowing were going to produce the future leaders of our church, the church that we never even knew we were going to plant! It's a valuable lesson to learn, you just never know what God is planning for the future, so do everything to the best of your ability.

God knew we were going to plant a church – we didn't. God knew that we were going to need a team that would stand by us through all the storms that would come our way. God knew that one of them might well be our future son-in-law. We had the privilege of 'raising' and mentoring Lorah's boyfriend Samuel, what a privilege, how many people get to do that?

How do you know whether or not the people that are in your life today aren't going to play a significant part of your future? You don't know, do you, but God does! One of the most important lessons that I learned was to do everything to the best of my ability and that included the way I invested in the people in my life. Our leadership team came out of our youth group and our connect group, the one where we pitched up each week, faithfully, just for one person - Dave.

Before we even began to appoint leaders or even think about a pastoral team, we set up our leadership structure. A structure that we felt could sustain us from a small church of twenty to any number, no matter how large we grew. Even though we didn't have anywhere near enough people to fill each role, we had a clear picture of what we were working towards and who we were looking for.

At first we tried to lead the church without giving anyone a title. We did this to try and avoid unnecessary arrogance and to avoid people who were looking for a title in our church, but in the end for various reasons, we allocated titles and job descriptions. Titles were more practical and clearly defined roles helped those serving to understand what was expected of them. Despite having a clear structure and detailed job descriptions for each role, we still held back for quite some time before appointing people to these roles. We had been burned by appointing the wrong people to lead when we first started the church and so we intended to be very careful before trusting people with our church again.

Paul gave Timothy some great advice when appointing leaders in church. Firstly he cautioned Timothy that a leader should *not be a novice, lest being puffed up with pride he fall into the same condemnation as the devil.*[10] Since our church consisted mainly of new

Christians it was difficult to find suitable leaders. It was also difficult to remember that they were new Christians because very often I would see their potential and quickly forget their lack of maturity. Many times I would have to force myself to remember that they simply lacked the years that were required to give them the maturity that they needed to lead.

Some Christians do grow faster than others but they all need a good few years under their belt before they have the wisdom to lead and to be able to cope with the pressure of leadership. And so, we reluctantly held off officially appointing any leaders in our church for quite some time, although most of the new Christians were very happily serving on a team in some capacity and more mature Christians were leading the teams without an official leadership title.

True leaders will lead with or without a title! A title is of no consequence to them and we were quickly able to identify which people were truly passionate about leading. The other bit of very helpful advice that Paul gave Timothy was not to *lay hands on anyone hastily*[11] and this was something that we adhered to.

And so our structure was agreed and some people were placed in boxes to test them out but no one was officially appointed leader for quite some time.

We decided that we needed a Senior Pastor and four assistant pastors - a Youth Pastor to care for under-twenties, a Community Pastor to take care of people and our community, a Creative Pastor to focus on the creative side of church and an Executive Pastor to handle the strategy and administration of the church. We allocated each pastor with three teams to manage.

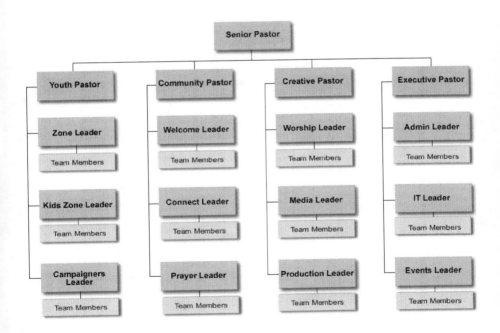

Eric and I led together as Senior Pastors and I took on an additional role as Executive Pastor as I had a good, strong background in this area. At first our team consisted of Eric, Dave and I along with a bunch of teenagers who were aged from fourteen to seventeen years old. As you can probably guess we were criticised! Some people who came to our church wondered why they, much older that seventeen, were not invited into our leadership team. Those who had been Christians for many years, some even having been to Bible School, wondered why they were not invited into the leadership team.

We were mocked, ridiculed and even had negative comments in the newspaper about our church. Eric and I never doubted the team we had chosen. They had faithfully served right from the beginning, in the days when we were a youth group, in the days where there was no title or prestige, just plain hard work. We knew their heart to serve and we had a special relationship with them. Age was not a deciding factor when choosing our core team and neither was education. A simple, proven passion for Jesus and His church and a willingness to do whatever it takes to build the church was all that was required along with a commitment to serve the leadership and vision of D7 Church one hundred percent.

Needless to say, all the people that criticised and complained stayed for a short time and then left to go to another church. It was always the 'old Christians' that had the most to say, did the least work and criticised the most. It was also the 'old Christians' that didn't agree with how we did things and left our church for greener pastures. However, it was that group of amazing teenagers that were always the first to pitch up at every single meeting, they were the first to roll up their sleeves and get on with the work come rain or shine and they were always the last people to complain.

In fact I can't remember a complaint from any of them. They loved the House of God, they served faithfully, they attended everything we asked of them loyally and there wasn't a day that we regretted appointing the core team that we did!

What guidelines can we give you when appointing your team? None! Sorry but we simply didn't follow any rules other than the obvious guidelines in

Timothy, we didn't measure them or weight them, we didn't fit them into any box. Actually it was more like they chose us. They would not go away; whenever we turned around they were right there beside us, loving Jesus and building His church!

Whenever we turned around they were there. Whenever we needed someone to help with something, they were right beside us. Yes, it is essential to build a great team around you when building a church and the best way to do that is probably just to include people into your personal life and see who sticks around. From there ask them to do some stuff in church and after that see who is still sticking around. Finally give them a tough challenge that will stretch them and if they are still sticking around then the chances are you will never be able to get rid of them and that makes for a great team!

One key we have found with people in general in our church is 'use them or lose them'. If people are ready to serve and they don't get used then they will find another places to get busy. Either it will be another church or they will find their way back to their sin. People like to feel useful, they need to be needed and when they serve in church they feel like they belong to something bigger than themselves. Even though our core team is very small, our team of helpers is very large. Almost ninety-five percent of our church serves on a team, anyone can get involved in some way, and we encourage it.

Our vision at D7 Church is the same as our discipleship program, which is the same as our mission statement – Belong, Believe, Serve. We win people to Jesus by getting them to belong through our connect groups and coffee area in the foyer on Sundays. Once they feel comfortable around us we either invite them into church or tell them about Jesus when the time is right. As soon as they are settled into church life, usually after coming for about three or four weeks in a row, we invite them to join a team. That is of course if they haven't already asked how they can get involved.

Many of our new Christians are so excited about church that they are practically begging us to do something in church! It's wonderful and we encourage them to get involved. We stick a broom in their hand or the coffee jug, we get them to help carry the boxes for setup or put up signage in the street. Our team has been trained to never turn someone away, even if it is an inconvenience, find something for an eager helper to do. Watch them while they help and if they show a particular skill or are consistent with their helping invite them to join a team.

There is no entry requirement to be on a team, which means that we have had some unusual team training nights. Lorah-Kelly did a fantastic job one Thursday evening as she spoke to the team about the importance of being clean and smelling good when coming to church. She also mentioned that it was not a good idea to have a smoke break at the front of church in a team T-shirt and that it probably wasn't a good idea to bring a can of beer to team night either! I deeply admired Lorah-Kelly that evening as she tackled a very difficult subject that most churches would not usually need to address at a team meeting. She did it while two of the team members were sipping on a beer and one of them had already clearly had one too many.

We laugh about times like these now but we do have to educate people about such basic things in our team because we welcome people off the street into our church and if they want to get involved we don't turn them away. Many people have come off drugs or alcohol as a result of being too busy at D7 Church to stay in touch with their old friends. We have even set up free music lessons for recovering addicts, where our band takes an hour a week to teach recovering addicts and anyone else who is interested, how to play an instrument or sing.

Robin, who came to our church off the street one Sunday, accepted Jesus on his very first visit to church. He was totally bowled over and couldn't stop saying how much he loved church and commented that he never knew that church was like this. We happened to have our baptisms that same day and invited Robin to be baptised. He accepted and was baptised right away. His passion for Jesus was contagious but he continued to struggle with alcohol.

It wasn't long after he was saved that he came along to our free music lessons and discovered his passion for keyboard and singing. Soon he was totally consumed with practicing music and less concerned with wasting away his time with drinking. Within six short months and many hours of practice, Robin has joined D7 Band and written his first song. I wouldn't be surprised if you hear his voice and songs on our next worship CD.

Know Your People

One of the most important things that I have learnt about building a team is the importance of taking your time to really know your people. There is little long term benefit to taking a person and putting them in a position to fill a gap for your benefit. Short term, this has benefits, stick someone whom you don't know into any position to suit you, do this to see their heart, to meet the church's needs and to begin the journey of discovering who they really are. There is a lot to learn from simply putting someone to work in any role at first.

If you leave them to stay there, it could be damaging and hinder them from reaching their God given potential. In our team, we allow people to move around, jump from team to team and to experiment with roles. Of course, they can't do this to the detriment of the team, but if opportunities are available to move and experiment we allow it at first, so that people can learn who they are and who they are not.

Recently we had a situation where Samuel, who had been with for us for a very long time and was given a great deal of freedom to experiment, was clearly in the wrong role. He displayed extreme passion and commitment to his role and seemed outwardly to be the right person for the job. But, we knew him **very well** and we saw that this role was not best for him. We had given him freedom to choose his team up to this point and supported him in his decisions, even though we were disappointed with his choice. Time had passed and we watched him in his role very closely. In his opinion, he was flourishing but in our opinion, he was not.

Often, what happens with people, is that they don't realise who they truly are because they become too familiar with what is a natural, God given talent. Samuel is extremely talented musically but he had chosen to lead the media and production team, he had even experimented with the IT Team. You couldn't fault him for his commitment, passion and determination but Eric and I were not convinced. We knew that his natural talent was music and we wanted him to take over the band, along with our daughter, Lorah-Kelly. Eventually we decided enough was enough. We had allowed him quite a long time to pursue the teams he wanted but we had to intervene for his own good.

It was crystal clear to us that Lorah-Kelly was the one with the natural artistic gift and having Samuel do graphics was not best for the team nor for Samuel. This is by no means a nasty thing to say and we would never have said this to Samuel in those words. But, if we didn't steer him in the right direction then both Lorah-Kelly and Samuel would have lost out on their God given destiny. We had prayed about it and made a decision that no matter what Samuel said, we were going to nudge him into the music role and get him to release the other teams he was currently leading.

Much to our surprise, he agreed. As soon as we mentioned what we wanted and the path that we wanted to put him on, he agreed. We were thrilled, now we could fast track another suitable person to lead the production team, we could get Lorah-Kelly to focus on the graphics and Samuel would focus on the talent that God had clearly given him.

Five people were significantly impacted because we made a decision based on what we **knew** to be true about Samuel. Firstly, Samuel flourished because he was working in the things that God had designed him to work in. Secondly, Lorah-Kelly was free to pursue her natural talent in the Media Team and thirdly, the new Production Team leader would rise up and become the man that God wanted him to be, as up to this point he had merely been in Samuel's shadow. Now that Samuel had stepped out of the way, the new leader could flourish.

Fourth and fifth were Eric and I, who greatly benefited from this change, as we were free to leave the band and focus on leading the church! For years Eric had played guitar in the band every single Sunday and jumped straight from the worship team into preaching. This exhausted him and he struggled each week to do his best with all that was required of him. When Eric left the band to Samuel, he was free to focus entirely on the message and the people, leaving the worship in Samuel and Lorah-Kelly's capable hands! I benefited too as I was far too busy on Sundays with leading worship and not able to focus on caring for Eric and for all the people in church.

Eric and I were free to allow Samuel and Lorah-Kelly to lead the band, because we **knew** them very well. We trusted them completely and had confidence in who they were becoming. It was a wonderful experience to finally have Samuel and Lorah-Kelly in the right place in church but it took a few years to train them and to get to know them and to find their God given role in our church. If we had not taken the time to really get to know Samuel and what God has put inside of him, we could be in a situation today where five people were left very frustrated, not reaching their full potential and not doing the things that God wanted them to do.

Chapter 8
Why Me?

Why Me?

2006 → 2007 → 2008 → 2009 → 2010 → **2011** →

"Am I on the wrong path, I have made a mistake! I am sure that I am not called to this. I am not good enough, I am not like all those other pastors who have it all figured out. I am certain God hasn't called me." Questions like these plagued me so often along with the big question, "Why me?"

I remember a dark, cold, winter's evening as Jordan (my fifteen year old daughter) and I went for a walk. We love to walk and talk. Well I love to walk and she loves to talk but on this rare occasion I got to do a little bit of talking too. Actually it was a bit of whining.

"Jordan I really don't think I am called to do this pastoring stuff. I am just not good enough!"

Jordan quickly interrupted before I even had a chance to get a good whinge out!

"Do I have to remind you about King David who was an adulterer and murderer? Or Moses – a murderer who couldn't speak properly? How about Gideon who was a complete wimp and used by God as a warrior! Need I go on?"

"Ok, yes, I see your point and I remember now. It's not about my weaknesses but it's about His strength."

We continued walking as I humbly shut up, knowing that she was totally right and also that she really didn't want to listen to my whining but wanted to talk about her current news. It's true though, isn't it? Why me? Why you? Well, why not? What qualifies us to do what God has called us to do? Nothing but God can truly qualify us. No university degree, no amount of Bible School and no amount of any spiritual activities qualifies us. God uses who He wants, when He wants and how He wants. There is no formula and no Biblical pattern that we can use to find out what qualifications are needed.

Weeks had passed since my conversation with Jordan. On this particular morning, I found myself holding onto a green metal fence at a park while light rain was slowly penetrating my t-shirt. Out of breath from my run, I pulled my leg up behind me as far as I could, to stretch out my muscles. As I held my stretch I heard the song words from Delirious that were melodically bellowing out of my headphones, "Here I am send me, here I am send me, there is nothing in my hands but here I am send me."

My eyes glazed over a bit as the words stung the deepest parts of my heart. As I contemplated my response to them the next chorus sang out, "Here I am send me, here I am send me, there is nothing in my hands but here I am send me."

Somehow I heard the words 'I am nothing' as clear as day instead of 'there is nothing in my hands'. I nodded in agreement thinking to myself that I am nothing and there is nothing in my hands but I painfully paused again at the thought of singing 'here I am send me'. I drifted off into a daze as I questioned the pain that I felt. It wasn't long before the next song, History Maker, started playing, at which point I turned off the music completely.

What happened to me? I used to sing these songs and other similar songs with such fervour, asking God so desperately to use me and send me and to do whatever He wanted with me. Tears streamed down my face as I walked towards my home. It wasn't that I was saying 'no' to God but at the same time I most certainly was not saying 'yes' in any shape, size or form! It was more like I was offering God a giant question mark.

Really God, do you really want to send me? I am nothing and have nothing and at this point want nothing.

My heart ached as I considered all the work I had done for God and how much hurt it had caused my tender heart, all the people that I had loved, even more deeply than my own family, and yet they chose to turn away from God to go down their own path again. All the money I had not been paid for my labours, all the financial sacrifices we had made as a family and all the time we had invested in this thing called church. It all seemed fruitless. The dream in my heart no longer cried out to God to send me or use me. Being a history maker no longer inspired me. To live to the end of my days without making any major mistakes seemed like the only reasonable goal left. What I used to dream of now seemed like a weight that I could no longer bear.

It was at that point that God interrupted my thoughts with a big "EXACTLY Angela!" He continued by reminding me that *His yoke is easy and His burden is light[12]*. I heard what He was saying but my heart was too damaged to receive it. So God continued to talk to me about how hard I had tried and how I had tried to build this church in my own strength. He pointed out that it has taken Him three years for Him to get me to this place where I would willingly give up the yoke that I was bearing.

Being the weaker vessel even applies to the things of God! I was never designed to carry this yoke called church; I was merely designed to do my small part. My head heard all of this truth but my heart was still hurting. I would never quit, that was not in my nature but I did not want my passion for church back. When I used to read David's word, "for *zeal for your house consumes me and the insults of those who insult you fall on me"[13]*, I used to think it was positive statement. Feeling as I did on that day I identified with it but more as a totally burnout statement. My zeal for God's House had consumed me, quite literally. I was completely used up, consumed!

The way forward presented itself and I knew things would be very different for me from that point forward. Jesus said, *"Take my yoke upon you and learn from me, for I am gentle and humble in heart, and you will find rest for your souls."[14]* Rest for my soul was what

I needed and the way to find it was to take His yoke and to learn from Him. I had no idea how this was going to work out practically but I started with a 'yes' to Him. I was not saying yes to 'send me' or yes to 'I want to be a history maker' or yes to 'use me'. My yes was only to accepting His yoke. I heard His sweet voice saying to me, *"Come to me, all you who are weary and burdened, and I will give you rest."*[15] And so I said yes to one thing and one thing only – rest!

'Why me?' was no longer a question I bothered asking, I knew that it didn't matter. I had nothing to offer that was useful to God at this point. Everything I thought I could offer Him had been consumed. No longer did I want to use my strength, no longer did I want to use my skill and no longer did I want to use my heart. I was empty, tired, hurt and alone in a journey that few people would ever understand.

Yes to rest, yes to His yoke was all I agreed to. The rest was up to Him now. Surrender truly was sweet. On a practical level this meant that I stopped most of what I was doing. Pitching up was my only commitment at this point. I would not start anything or build anything or lead anything, I would only commit to pitching up. Leaders meetings, church on Sunday, social events if necessary were still on the agenda; however, I pulled back from **making** anything happen. *I got out of bed, I breathed in and out*[16] and I pitched up.

Everything inside of me wanted to stay home, stay in bed and hide away. I knew that if I did that I would do more damage than good. I had done my part by pitching up and putting my body at the right place and on time – the rest was up to God. I could only offer Him an empty vessel, which I think He preferred anyway. I am sure I could hear all of heaven sighing saying, "Finally, a vessel we can use." As John so aptly put it, *"He must become greater; I must become less.*[17]*"*

Why me? Well, certainly not because I was great or that I had much to give. Probably because I was becoming less so that He could become greater, both in and through me. *For in him we live and move and have our being*[18], something that I was only beginning to understand. That day, after my run and revelation at the green fence, my heart leapt with hope. Hope that I could move forward, not hope that I could do more. Hope that my heart would feel again but this time with His heart beating inside of me.

My hope was in His promise, *"I will give you a new heart and put a new spirit in you; I will remove from you your heart of stone and give you a heart of flesh."*[19] My hope was that He was going to do the work in me and I no longer had to keep doing the work in my own strength. The New Living Translation says it like this, *"And I will give you a new heart, and I will put a new spirit in you. I will take out your stony, stubborn heart and give you a tender, responsive heart"* I had to chuckle because I realised that I had been quite stony and stubborn most of my life.

Finally, I heard His sweet voice say that I no longer needed to be strong but that I could be weak so that He could be strong. He said that *I could do all this through him who gives me strength*[20]. So I rested and I waited but I continued to pitch up.

Chapter 9
It's Not About You

It's Not About

You

It's simple! It's not about you. It never was and it never will be. It's not your church, it's His church and it's not your will, it's His will. He had the blueprint and He will build the church according to His plans and purposes. There is very little that you can actually do that will make it work or that can make it grow unless He is building it. You can work your fingers to the bone, you can love all the people in your world, you can do whatever you think is possible, but if He is not building it then it is all in vain. *Unless the LORD builds the house, they labour in vain who build it[21].*

Plainly put – we can't **make** church happen. To be honest, we really shouldn't want to anyway. None of us are designed to carry such a heavy burden and none of us can. Most importantly, God should get all the glory for His church. If man can do it then man will become proud and ultimately wreck it. As mentioned before, God never chose you because of your skill or special talents. It's more likely that he chose you because of your weakness or because of your teachable spirit.

Vashti

The book of Esther is a fantastic book about how a woman saved the Jewish people but there is so much more to that story than first meets the eye. There is the story of Vashti!

A long, long time ago, in a country called Persia, there lived a powerful king named Ahasuerus (aHa-shoo-eerus) who ruled over a vast empire of one hundred and twenty seven provinces which spread all the way from India to Ethiopia. He ruled in his magnificent fortified palace along with his a beautiful queen named Vashti.

During his reign, King Ahasuerus wanted to show off to his entire kingdom, so he held a feast. *He showed the riches of his glorious kingdom and the splendour of his excellent majesty for many days, one hundred and eighty days in all[22].* It seems that this extravagant feast still hadn't proven enough so he followed it with another feast for every single person in the county, *from great to small, in the court of the garden of the king's palace[23].*

Still, despite all the showing off, he still didn't seem to be satisfied, so he called for his beautiful queen so he could show her off too. The King sent seven of his finest men, *to show her beauty to the people and the officials, for she was beautiful to behold. But Queen Vashti refused to come at the king's command brought by his eunuchs; therefore the king was furious, and his anger burned within him[24].*

The King was so baffled that he asked the seven highest ranking princes in his kingdom to advise him! He asked them; *"What shall we do to Queen Vashti, according to law, because she did not obey the command of King Ahasuerus brought to her by the eunuchs?"[25]*

One of the King's top men called Memucan answered;

"Queen Vashti has not only wronged the king, but also all the princes, and all the people who are in all the provinces of King Ahasuerus. For the queen's behaviour will become known to all women, so that they will despise their husbands in their eyes, when they report, 'King Ahasuerus commanded Queen Vashti to be brought in before him, but she did not come.' This very day the noble ladies of Persia and Media will say to all the king's officials that they have heard of the behaviour of the queen. Thus there will be excessive contempt and wrath.

If it pleases the king, let a royal decree go out from him, and let it be recorded in the laws of the Persians and the Medes, so that it will not be altered, that Vashti shall come no more before King Ahasuerus;

and let the king give her royal position to another who is better than she.

When the king's decree which he will make is proclaimed throughout all his empire (for it is great), all wives will honour their husbands, both great and small." And the reply pleased the king and the princes, and the king did according to the word of Memucan.[26] And so it was that Vashti was out and a new Queen was to be chosen.

Now let's consider Vashti's position. Her drunken husband called for her to come and parade around in front of his drunken friends and all of the people that were in the king's palace so that he could prove how powerful and wonderful he was. Her response in modern English probably went like this, "Hell no! Do you really think I am going to be humiliated in front of all of your drunken friends? No thank you! I am staying here with my girlfriends to finish our dinner party; I will see you when you sober up."

I am not sure how accurate my interpretation of her response is but I am pretty sure that she felt justified no matter how she presented her response. To be honest, I thought about this over and over again and thought that I would probably do the same thing under those circumstances. As I pondered on Vashti's response and on the beauty of Esther, I realised that there must be a reason why her response was so unacceptable. The Bible would not have recorded the book of Esther as a good thing if an injustice was done against Vashti.

As I considered Vashti as a leader I realised that I was not very different from her and the things that I perceived to be wrong in her leadership were in fact also wrong in my leadership. Humble pie was what I had to swallow before being able to admit to the things I am about to admit to!

Count the Cost & Pay the Price

Firstly, if you desire to be a leader you desire a good thing[27] but with leadership comes a great deal of responsibility, *for everyone to whom much is given, from him much will be required; and to whom much has been committed, of him they will ask the more*[28].

You see, when you desire to lead you have to count the cost and make sure you are able to finish what you started. *For which of you, intending to build a tower, does not sit down first and count the cost, whether he has enough to finish it— lest, after he has laid the foundation, and is not able to finish, all who see it begin to mock him, saying, 'This man began to build and was not able to finish'?*[29]

I have no idea if Vashti counted the cost to becoming queen before she became the queen, but I can see that she didn't pay the price of being a queen when it needed to be paid. A queen is a public servant, her life is no longer her own, her life becomes a life that serves the public. It's a high price to pay and every decision needs to be carefully considered as the results will not only affect her but there will be a chain reaction through the people that she leads. In Vashti's case, the king's advisors cautioned him that the chain reaction from Vashti's simple 'no' would cause all the women in his kingdom to think that they too could treat their husbands in this manner.

Perhaps Vashti was justified as a wife to dislike her husband's request to parade around in her royal robes at the drunken party, but as a queen, as a leader, it was more important that she considered the example she was setting! Personally I find this a tough call, but I realise that if I want to be a leader then these are the sort of decisions I will have to face. It's not about me but it's about the example I am setting and the precedent I am setting for the people who look up to me. Today's permissions are tomorrow's standards! This is the cost of leadership, you are no longer your own, you are on permanent display and you are permanently setting an example. People are watching you ALL the time, most of the time they are copying you and some of the time they are judging you. Let's be real for a moment, it's flippin' tough! At the same time it's important to understand that you will make mistakes, I make mistakes all the time. The key though, is how you deal with those mistakes.

I remember once when I was in a very stressful situation I started snapping at a team member in church. He was annoying me and he was being rude to me. One thing that rubs me up the wrong way is when people don't show respect to older people and to leaders. I was both to this person, he was young and he was a team member and he showed me no respect! So I snapped at him in front of everyone. Although I realised that he probably deserved a bit of correction I also realised that I might have humiliated him in front of his team members. I had made a mistake. I was wrong to snap at him, especially in front of everyone. As soon as I realised this I made a point of apologising to him in front of the same people I humiliated him in front of. I told him I was wrong and I said I was sorry.

It wasn't easy. In fact it was painful to have to do that especially in front of everyone but I knew that everyone was watching me ALL the time. I also knew that I had an opportunity to set an example to all that were present. If I learned to apologise when I made a mistake then they would see how it was done. They too would make mistakes so I was able to model to them how to deal with it.

It wasn't long after that incident that the same person who I had snapped at was a bit rude to me again. A couple of weeks after this incident, he came over and apologised to me in exactly the same manner that I had apologised to him weeks earlier. I know for sure that this was out of character for him and the only reason he apologised was because he learned from the example I had set for my team.   Vashti didn't set a good example and so she was banished.

You have to constantly be asking yourself this question, "Am I building people and making them bigger than me or am I using people to make myself and my ministry bigger?"   It's so easy to get passionate about making the church bigger and more amazing but if you are doing it at the expense of people then you are building nothing. Building people is building the church!

Chapter 10
Let God be God

Let God be God

2006 ▸ 2007 ▸ 2008 ▸ 2009 ▸ 2010 ▸ **2011** ▸

"D7 is a warm, happy and friendly church to belong to. At D7 we have seen some really lost people find God and we have seen God transform these lives before our eyes. It's so beautiful.

We have made new friends from different backgrounds but we all have one very important thing in common- a deep love for God. D7 has become a part of our family and a big part of our lives."

- *Tamara Farmer, D7 Church*

It is easy to say let God be God but allowing Him to be God is another story. Well it was for me anyway! You see I have always been the sort of person that had things nice and tidy and in order. It was my nature to be organised and this was not necessarily a bad thing. Organisation is a part of the administrative gifting that God has given me but it became a problem when I had things so organised that there was no room for God to move.

After becoming aware of this, I began to ask God how to let go and allow Him some room in our life, especially church life since it was His church after all. It was a long, slow process where I started letting go of things and realising that without them I could still survive.

For example, one of my responsibilities was to keep a church blog updated with all the week's activities. Several people were subscribed and they relied on the weekly email from the blog, to see what was going on in the life of the church during each week. This was a small job but one of the little things that added to the pile of many things that I did. At the beginning of 2011 I made a commitment to cut out unnecessary things and to focus on just one thing for the entire year and that was to invest in the women in our church.

I shut down the blog and guess what? The church didn't fall apart, in fact nothing changed. It might have been a nice little comfort for people but all that work for something that wasn't essential was truly a waste of my time. Once I realised the importance of my focus, I shut down other things that I was doing in church too, again only to discover that life still carried on. This process was very liberating and the time that I gained was essential for a successful year ahead. God was slowly becoming God in my life and I was realising that I didn't have to have everything under control all the time.

We had noticed a similar pattern in the team. Everyone was doing a great job with their team, their work was great but we were concerned that they had forgotten the reason behind their task. It was as if they were pitching up for church and going through the motions to get the job done. It was fair to say that if we were a secular organisation that didn't serve God it would have made no difference.

This thought frightened us so we took action. We declared a fast! For twenty-one days in January, we asked the whole church to join us in a Daniel fast. Our prayer was that God would renew the joy of our salvation[30]. If God was not God in our church then we were in a lot of trouble. There was no point in continuing until God was put in His rightful place in our hearts and in our church. Our fast not only consisted of abstaining from food but also abstaining from work. We cancelled all teams on the three Sundays during the fast. There was to be no work in church!

On the first Sunday of the fast it was quite a challenge to get everyone to do nothing except worship God and listen to the word. We INSISTED that there was no sound and lighting, no coffee or sandwiches in the foyer, no Kids Zone and no Welcome Team. Eric and I lead worship with an acoustic guitar and vocals and we recorded the service on a mobile phone on the pulpit.

We printed the song lyrics onto a piece of paper the old-fashioned way and handed them out at church.

It was very difficult to explain to the congregation and to the visitors why we were even eliminating the sandwiches and coffee that we usually gave to the homeless people that visited our church on Sunday. It didn't make sense to many but we knew that this fast was essential. A few weeks without sandwiches and coffee was not going to kill anyone but a church where God is not God could kill us all. It was a very hard but very necessary decision.

By the second Sunday during the fast the team had accepted how things were and they didn't argue with us about the work. By the third Sunday we noticed that although there was no Welcome Team, everyone took it upon themselves to mingle and welcome new people. We also noticed that although there was no sound system, fancy lighting or media on the screen, people still worshipped God. In fact for the first time ever, I actually noticed more than a handful of people worshipping – usually people were sat around chatting at the back and others spent their time focused on their task. This Sunday was the first Sunday, ever, that I felt we were actually worshipping God.

It was beautiful! A part of me wanted to keep things this way forever. I loved the simple, pure, uncomplicated adoration of our God. We did go back to church as usual at the end of our fast with all the modern gizmos and cool things. Our heart was changed though and our values were reset. God was put back on the throne and the team knew that if we fell back into the trap of loving the work and not the God that we do the work for, then we would ditch the teams again and refocus.

I sincerely don't believe God is interested in all that stuff. God will honour us with His presence when He finds a church that is waiting for Him, a church that longs for His presence, a church that knows that without Him, as God of their life, there is no life at all. It was only after this fast that we started to grow in numbers. Also, it was only after this fast, that we began to grow in spiritual hunger. We no longer valued all the stuff but we began a journey of valuing God, His presence, His Holy Spirit and the precious sacrifice of Jesus.

Preaching the pure Bible became our passion too rather than preaching clever, funny, motivational messages to entertain people. We became hard-core! Lives were being wasted in our city,   people literally dying from drug abuse, children being taken away from their parents, young women turning to prostitution. If you wanted to see the need it wasn't that hard to find. Most people walk around our city with blinkers on because they want to deny that there is a problem. If they admitted that there was a problem they would have to do something about it, so people were blind by choice. Sadly, even many churches have adopted the blinkers too.

With God as God of our church, we had no blinker option. If we wanted His presence amongst us we needed to reach out to the least and the smallest.

Chapter 11

Raise Leaders

Raise Leaders

2006 → 2007 → 2008 → 2009 → 2010 → **2011** →

A while ago, I heard someone say, "If you're leading but no one is following then you're just taking a walk."

Letting Go

One thing I have learned is that it's good to keep people under your wing and to help them grow into the leaders they need to be. The nurturing, mothering side of me comes naturally when raising leaders too. This is all good but if done for too long can be harmful. There comes a time when the babies need to be released. A good leader will know when to hold on and they will know when to let go. In life, there are so many illustrations of this.

Take a baby for example. If a parent held onto the baby while learning to walk then the baby would never walk alone, they would remain dependant. It is only once the parent actually lets go of the baby that the baby manages to walk. I can guarantee you that for every parent the experience is the same, when letting go, the child falls after taking a few steps. It's the same with raising leaders; they won't get it right first time. Once you let go you have to accept that there will be a process before they can confidently walk alone.

In the animal kingdom, baby birds leave the nest before they can fly. They need some time to get used to the ground, hopping around and climbing on low branches. Their wings need to develop so they use this time to exercise their wings until they are strong enough for flight. The parent birds continue to feed and care for the little ones that cannot yet fly, until they are self-sufficient. Again, this is something we need to do both when raising Christians and when raising leaders too.

It's essential to get the trainee leader out of their comfort zone so that they grow independent. At the same time it's always good to keep a close eye on them and watch over them while they are 'finding their feet'. The worst thing that can happen to a potential leader is that the one training them never lets go. This would be the equivalent of a baby not ever learning to walk or a bird living in the nest all through adulthood and never learning to fly.

I have heard of leaders that keep people dependant so that they can feel good about themselves. One of my good friends was severely damaged by this sort of poor leadership. This is insecure leadership, a sort of leadership that is extremely dangerous and an easy trap to fall into. The sign of a good leader is when they do themselves out of a job or when all the people around them have grown bigger than themselves. Now that is the sort of leader that Eric and I want to be. We want everyone on our team to be better than us and we won't be satisfied until we have a dynamic team of leaders that can go on without needing us anymore.

Chapter 12
Lead by Example

Lead by

Example

2006 → 2007 → 2008 → 2009 → 2010 → **2011** →

I watched with amazement! Some new street people had arrived for a free cup of coffee and sandwich. This was usual on Sundays as we set up our foyer to attract the broken, smelly, hungry people from the street.   It was often uncomfortable as some of the people that came in were quite scary looking and you never knew if they were there to do harm, to steal from us for drug money or to harm our children. I watched with the eye of a hawk over our little ones as this group of rough looking people walked up towards the coffee machine.

They were greeted with a big smile by one of our congregation, offered a sandwich and shown to a table. I continued to watch with amazement as this person, new to church, sat down at the table with them and began to initiate a conversation. When their coffee and sandwich was finished, he (or she?) offered them more and continued in a conversation with our guests. At one point, they all burst out in laughter but I wasn't close enough to hear the joke. I sensed a good vibe from that table.

My heart was filled with joy! It was happening! The culture in our church was strong. We hadn't taught this to the new people that had recently joined our church. We hadn't uttered a word to them yet about how we did things in our church.   They had simply observed and copied what they had observed. I was thrilled as I witnessed the first 'batch' of new church members simply get on with it!

It hadn't always been this way. Eric, Dave, Lorah-Kelly and I had laboured hard for nearly two years doing all the loving and caring ourselves along with a handful of people that we kept close to us. Our team had remained small over these past months even though we tried everything within our power to add to our numbers. Every Thursday we had met with the same eight people, teaching and training intensively so that they would in turn teach and train their team members when their teams grew.

There were times when we thought they would never get it and that the team would simply never grow but one thing encouraged us! They kept pitching up. Every Sunday, every Thursday and whenever else we needed them, the same group of people would pitch up – they would ALWAYS be there. And so we continued to mould them and share our dreams and passion with them.

The Sunday that I mentioned at the beginning of this chapter did not have one of these eight people serving the tables though. Our team of eight were all busy doing what they were trained to do, they were busy setting up the building for our church service, making coffee and organising the children. Our team were doing an excellent job in getting everything ready and the new trainees were in the foyer serving the guests. As I watched with amazement I realised that the reason they were doing this is because this is what Eric and I do every Sunday. We leave the team to get on with the technical stuff so that we can meet and greet guests. Ideally we should have had a stronger welcome team to do that but because we had only eight people on team we had to take care of the guests ourselves. Lorah-Kelly and Dave also joined in with welcoming guests as soon as they had their areas set up. The result was that the four key leaders of the church were the ones having coffee with guests.

Before you think that I am writing this for applause please know that my heart is only to show you what we have noticed on our journey. We never once set out to be seen to be greeting the guests or to be seen hugging smelly people. It was purely out of necessity and passion for our church that we ended up doing these things.

Looking back now though, I can honestly say that this is exactly what leaders should be doing by choice. You see, our new church members were imitating us. We didn't need to have a training session on how to love street people. Leading by example was probably the most powerful training session possible. We didn't have to say one word to anyone, we simply did the exact thing that we wanted them to do and without realising it started to create a powerful culture in our church. Everything that we have done has been copied by our people. We open our home regularly and cook for people and now other people have started doing the same. We pack our car to full capacity and drive people home after church or pick them up for church and now other people have started doing the same! We hug people, even though some of them smell worse than a toilet bowl. We shake hands with men that have visible dirt on their hands and under their fingernails. We have even on occasion allowed people to hug our children if the children were comfortable.

Most importantly of all, we have take the time to listen to peoples stories and we have wept unashamedly and publicly as they tell us about their child that died or the abuse they have endured or how they desperately want to get free from drugs but can't find a way out. Often we sit in the foyer before the worship begins and simply listen. Then when we have to leave to go into the auditorium, we invite them to join us for church. If they decline, we exchange phone numbers and tell them that we will call them during the week and we do make that call during the week! This is what we, the leaders of our church do, and so this is what we can expect the members of the church to do too. If we weren't able to do it ourselves then we should not feel comfortable expecting others to do it.

There might come a day when we are not always available to be in the foyer as we might find ourselves pulled to one side for a private conversation or to deal with a set-up issue. On these occasions I have no doubt whatsoever that the atmosphere in the foyer will remain one of genuine love for each and every person that walks through our doors. It was hard work at first when this atmosphere depended only on us but it was a price that was worth paying. I can honestly say that you cannot teach this sort of thing, you have to model it; you have to lead by example.

Another area where we have led by example is in the area of how men and women treat each other, again unintentionally, but we have noticed the fruit and have observed ourselves! Our marriage has set the tone in our church for how men and women speak to each other and how they treat each other. Our daughters have set high standards for dating in our church and we are so grateful that they are a part of this journey with us. These things have only come to our attention when we hear a young man say to a young woman the exact words that Eric and I say to each other! It's quite frightening when you realise how much influence you really do have as a leader.

Sadly, this influence works both ways, so it is essential to point out quickly to your church when you have made a mistake and apologise. After the apology should come a suggestion for what should have happened in place of the mistake. This is very humbling but leading by example does include these moments of humility too. People like leaders that they can relate to and many pastors feel that they need to be perfect to lead. Their congregation can't relate to them as it's impossible to be perfect, so they don't receive what the pastor is trying to say as freely as they should. Sadly, these pastors do make mistakes but try to cover them up. People see this and feel more disillusioned than ever.

Leading by example means making mistakes too, keeping it real and staying humble for the sake of the people you are influencing. I remember on one occasion I was really stressed! We were doing an outdoors event, the setup was just not going according to plan, and so I spoke very harshly to one of the young team members! I felt justified in doing so because he just wasn't listening to what I was telling him to do. As I walked away, probably to have a go at someone else, I heard the quiet voice of God telling me to apologise. Ouch, that didn't feel nice. He also told me to apologise publicly, in front of the same people that were there in the first place. I didn't like this! I hate being wrong anyway and to admit I was wrong in front of a group of people was going to hurt badly.

But I trusted God. I walked over to the young man and said that I was wrong to be so harsh and I was very sorry. I also went on to make an excuse that I was just a bit stressed. That was my little addition to what God told me to do and I really should have left that part out. I know it's terrible to justify your actions after an apology, but I am still working on that!

A few weeks later that same young man came up to me at church and apologised to me for snapping at me that morning during set up. He also went on to justify his actions. I was dumbfounded. It was not in this young man's nature to admit he was wrong and I had never heard him apologise before in my life either. Immediately the Holy Spirit reminded me of the incident a few weeks earlier and showed me how he was copying my example, down to the very last detail! Perhaps if I had not added my little justification on to the end of my apology then he would not have done so too when he apologised to me.

This little seemingly insignificant experience was life changing for me and since then I have worked diligently at being transparent in leading by example both by my good works that I hope will inspire others to imitate but also in my mistakes. Making a mistake is not necessarily a bad thing if it can be used to teach and to help people gain character. I have used this with my children too. If I am wrong I go to them and admit what I have done wrong and I apologise to them and ask for forgiveness.

I have realised that I am a leader and whatever I do will be copied by those I lead. It's not so much about what I say but it is always about what I do. In fact, what I say is received through the filter of what I do and if the people I lead don't respect what I do, then they will most certainly not listen to what I have to say.

Chapter 13
Money

Money

2006 → 2007 → 2008 → 2009 → 2010 → **2011** →

Church and money, an interested combination! It shouldn't be such a big deal, God owns the church and He owns all the silver and all the gold[31]. So why then do so many people associate churches with poverty?

Our church has done some pretty wild stuff that costs loads of money and we did it with a starting point of zero pounds. It all started, well, when the church started. We started the church with no money and only one of our core team was employed at the time and even he was struggling financially, so basically none of us had any money.

Our first hurdle with no money was to start the church. We needed instruments for the band and sound equipment. Our bank balance was at the afore-mentioned starting point of zero. We prayed, we asked God for money and gear and then we got on with the other preparations for the big launch day. It wasn't long before we were given one thousand pounds for our church plant from someone outside of our church, who had heard about what we were doing. It was fantastic; we were able to buy a guitar and amp and a bass guitar and amp. Before long someone donated a drum kit to us and soon afterwards someone bought speakers, a mixing desk and other necessary bits for the church. We had everything that we needed, thousands of pounds worth of equipment. After all this activity our bank balance returned very close to zero.

Church life continued, God met all of our needs, both great and small but then we got tired. Our personal bank balance was around zero but I knew that if I didn't have a break I would die... or get very close. It was urgent, I couldn't wait. I asked God for a holiday for our family and then I immediately booked a week away. Our bank balance was zero but I knew that God knew that we needed this break so I took the 'chance'. I would like to say I had faith but honestly it was a hope, a risk with a touch of faith sprinkled on top. Three days after booking the holiday someone came to our home to give us one thousand pounds towards a holiday as they had noticed how tired our family was! WOW! Fantastic! It was awesome, there was no need to even scrape pennies together for ice-cream for the kids, and we had enough for a good family break with all the nice trimmings.

Life and church carried on after our wonderful, all expenses paid holiday but we hit a point where we needed a bit of a spiritual boost. No problem, with our bank at the usual close to zero balance, we were given an all expenses paid short break to a London church conference. Fantastic! Hotel paid for, food paid for, conference ticket paid for and transport paid for. It was a life changing few days. Months passed and even though it was fantastic and we learned essential leadership lessons, we were feeling physically tired again.

No problem for God! Once again, with the usual zero plus a few pennies in the bank, Eric and I were given an all expenses paid holiday to the USA for two weeks. It was incredible, we rested and rested and rested until we could rest no more. This was in December after a long year of hard work. God's timing was perfect as He knew what the next year had in store for us, He knew we would need that boost to get through the year ahead - a year that had no holidays in it!

And so we pressed on but church finances got really tight. For some reason we weren't making it with our income and expenses every month, our income came up a bit short for our modest expenses. We prayed and brainstormed creative ways to deal with the problem. The plan was that we would spend every second Sunday out in the community. Our awesome D7 Band played in the city square and in the park every second Sunday during the entire summer. It was loads of fun and we saved plenty of money on venue hire in order to keep our church going. This may not seem like God's provision to you but actually, He did something incredible through this. You see, at times God doesn't provide. Not because He can't but because if He did we would head in the opposite direction to what He wants. His provision is ALWAYS perfect; our understanding of His provision is what is often flawed.

It was during this summer that God had a plan for us that we were oblivious to. During one of our 'gigs' in the city square someone came up to us and asked us if they could buy one of our CDs. We laughed inside but on the outside politely said that we don't have one available *yet*. A few more weeks passed and we were approached by an influential person in Gloucester who was impressed with our music. He invited us to play at an upcoming city event and then in passing mentioned that we should bring our CDs with us to sell on the day.

Yes, it was becoming obvious to us that we needed to put our awesome music onto CD. The following week, with a very close to zero bank balance of course, I made an appointment to see a music producer.

He gave us a quote to record and produce our CD and we shook hands and agreed on a date and a price. Yes, we shook hands knowing full well that we had a zero bank balance but I did tell him that we wanted to pay in advance. We might not have a huge bank balance but I was adamant that I would never lead our church into debt, so we paid for things up front, I just felt safer that way.

Within one week we had the one thousand five hundred pounds that we needed to record our CD. It was an exciting time and everyone in the band had never experienced anything like it before. God's provision was perfect. If He wanted to, He could have provided money for our venue hire just like He had provided for all the other needs on our journey, but He didn't. He knew that if He forced us out into the community we would do much better than when we were neatly tucked away in our comfortable venue.

Not only did we make important connections with influential people in our city but we also managed to preach the gospel to people that would not necessarily step into a church building.

King's Daughters Conference

As with all the things that God has done through us, King's Daughters was no different, it just kind of happened. Looking back over the years I can see God's careful planning of this ministry and I can see all the training and preparation He had given me, but at the time it didn't seem significant at all.

King's Daughters, the women's ministry in D7 Church, started as a blog. I felt too embarrassed to have a blog that was about me with my name as the title. I tried to start an "Angela De Souza" Facebook page but I didn't feel right about promoting myself, so I changed that name to King's Daughters too. It wasn't long before my blog grew from a little bit of family news to the place where I taught and encouraged the women in our church. It was also from my blog that the King's Daughters Conference was conceived.

I never intended for it to happen and never had any desire to lead women or host a women's conference, but as I said previously, it had always been there deep down inside of me. God had been preparing me my whole life for *such a time as this,* only I had no idea!

My desire to tell women who they really are grew into an obsession to reach women and help them find freedom in who God made them to be. Here follow the ramblings of a woman 'pregnant' with a conference.

January 2011

First Trimester (1 to 12 weeks)

It was unplanned! I had no intention of getting 'pregnant' and I most certainly wasn't trying to - it just happened. I sat considering the year ahead and felt that this was the year to focus on building something for the women. Until this point I had never felt the time was right, but now, on this day, it felt right. So I opened my heart and wrote down a few ideas on my blog.

I started off with a Girls Night! It seemed like a fun idea and didn't look like too much work. The focus was very specifically to disciple and care for the girls in our church. It was not to be a time of outward focus and reaching out to the lost, this was very much about growing the girls inside our church into beautiful, Godly women.

Every Tuesday night, at my home, we had a nice time together over a lovely dinner. The focus of our Girl's Night was to get closer to each other and closer to God, so that we could be all that God wanted us to be. We spent time chatting about real life stuff, we prayed for each other and cared for each other. For special occasions we planned to dress up and go out somewhere fancy - just for fun! Our theme was to explore the big question for 2011 - "What is the true meaning of being a woman?"

Slowly the focus shifted - I couldn't see myself only having an inward focused group - we needed to be beautiful, Godly women for a purpose. When the girls grew a little, my plan was to offer them an opportunity to reach out to the lost and dying world around them, and to share what they had gained in our Girl's Nights.

Girl's Friday Nights would become a monthly girl's night with a sharp focus to reach out to women in our community who are struggling with life and who are far from God. Our cities are filled with lonely, hurting woman who are desperate for solutions in their life and before King's Daughters attempts to have a global impact we must first have a local impact. As always we would have great fun nights but these nights were specifically set aside for us to reach out to others, starting with our neighbours and people we meet daily, as well as women trapped in detention centres, prostitution, asylum, single parenthood and so many other things.

Conception

Then it happened, the conference was conceived. I had no idea that I had conceived a conference, I just wrote a few random thoughts down on my blog. It seemed like a good idea so why not? I thought nothing of it and added these thoughts to the line up for the year. I wrote,

"An exciting look at what can happen when a woman places her ordinary life into the hands of an extraordinary God! King's Daughters exists to inspire and challenge women to understand their identity and value so that they can lead an amazing, abundant life with passion and purpose. The King's Daughters Conference is a unique

experience where you will encounter God, be completely refreshed and equipped to be all you can possibly be."

Words flowed with ease onto my blog and the date was set. I didn't think anything of it and got on with my year.

Early Signs of Pregnancy

Tiredness consumed me. My usual energetic, perky, self-motivated self had become a very tired heap of 'nothing'. Nothing inspired me, nothing motivated me and nothing interested me. Some days I was even scared, wondering what had happened to me. How did I go from the high that I was on last year to this exhausted, tired, very low woman? Something was wrong but I didn't know what.

After careful examination I determined that I was not depressed. I still had my joy and I still loved life. Hope was still in place and there was nothing that I wanted to change. I was simply tired! Little did I know that this was one of the most common early signs of pregnancy. I almost forgot about the conference until one day when I started dabbling with the events page on my blog again. The idea started to tug at me and I thought perhaps this would actually happen.

Confirmation of Pregnancy

Randomly, out of the blue, one of our congregation came up to me after I preached one Sunday, and said, "That was a conference message young lady!"

I was very surprised. Of all the things he could have said, why *those words*. He had no idea of the plans I had made or the desires of my heart. Even I didn't fully realise the desires of my heart until he said those words. Of course! Of course it's a conference message. I found myself delighted and excited and ready to make firm plans to do this conference that I had so boldly written about. The pregnancy test had been done and the pregnancy was now confirmed. I could no longer deny that there was something growing inside of me.

Within days the tiredness started lifting and the excitement grew. It was official now - I was doing a women's conference in September - nine months after conception. At the time, of course, I didn't count the months, it was only upon reflection that I realised the significant timeline.

April

Second trimester (13 to 27 weeks)

Busyness and frantic planning had left little to write about during this trimester. All I can say is that I was extremely excited with occasional patches of nervousness. Most of the time I simply busied myself with the preparations for this big day!

August

Third trimester (28 to 40 weeks)

It was August with about four weeks to go and I felt so tired! I felt like I was carrying a heavy weight around with me all the time. Everything felt like such hard work. I had only sold three tickets and was hoping to have sold one hundred by this point. I felt like giving up so many times but the nagging 'what ifs' were my constant companion. What if it all worked out at the last minute? What if God was testing my faith and I failed by quitting? What if lives were depending on this? So I held on and kept pushing forward. I didn't want to wish my life away but I did really wish it was the 11th September or the 12th, or any day AFTER the conference! Each day seemed so tiring and so stressful. When I was not worrying about ticket sales I was remembering that I had to preach two messages and host the whole thing. That was even scarier than the ticket sales! So I ignored it and stayed focused on the details of the conference, the things that I could control!

9 September 2011

It was the day before the due date, I had done all that I could do, all that was within my control. The rest was up to God!

10 September 2011

D-day had arrived! Nothing was going according to plan, set up was late, guests had not arrived yet, we were five minutes away from starting and the sound was not working! Panic hit me, I was sure it was going to flop, everything was going wrong.

It was out of my control, there was nothing I could do so I decided just to get through the day and whatever happened happened. Needless to say it happened! We had a fantastic day. Once we actually managed to start, everything flowed perfectly and I had so much fun! Never did I imagine that I could actually enjoy the day too. We pulled it off! Our awesome team actually pulled off a top notch conference with no money, no experience or clue of what to expect. We pulled off an exceptional day, a day which was nearly cancelled several times for various reasons. Money was the biggest 'reason' to cancel but we pressed on, then lack of helpers was another reason but we pressed on, more reasons to cancel cropped up but we pressed on and I am so glad we did. Read some of the feedback from the very first King's Daughters Conference,

"The Conference was AWESOME!
Such an amazing day, I will be remembering this all year.
The speakers were just amazing, they were so real and
talked about everyday issues that all women face today
and it was just amazing to hear their stories. The food

was DELICIOUS! The guys serving were awesome and the band playing was wonderful. Kings Daughters Conference was a truly breathtaking experience; I cannot wait for next year! xxx"

"Today was fantastic! I found hope and new life. To everyone who helped and served you were all amazing and I can't wait till next year!"

"Friday night I was ready to quit on life. It took everything I had in me to not do something silly. I knew I would lose everything if I did. I cried saying that I want to feel normal and not like a freak in my own body - to feel worthy and accepted. Everything that was spoken on Saturday at the conference touched every fibre of my being. I am so glad I came, I feel reborn! xxxx"

"I just wanted to say again how blessed I was at the Kings Daughters Conference. God really touched and blessed me. Please give my thanks to ABSOLUTELY aLL who took part on that day....those dear men who dressed up for us... to whom nothing was too much

trouble/the beautiful presentations/butterflies/cakes, etc.... IT WAS A TOTALLY BEAUTIFUL DAY and I am just beginning to feel something of God's beauty is in me too. Bless God. The talks were just so helpful/encouraging that we heard that you wonderful women had struggles and how God was walking through all this.....creating beauty from ashes, newness, healing and restoration. Inspiring and yes gave hope...so part of that promise across the screen at the beginning from Jeremiah...future and hope. Oh...that beginning was fantastic....Holy Spirit began to work right through that....and the welcome. I think you get the picture...I was blessed and so please all accept a big thank you."

"Very well done for yesterday. We had so much fun and we were so blessed."

Imagine if we had cancelled! All those lives changed, all that fun had, the entire experience for so many people would never have happened if we had looked at the spreadsheet detailing the money. I immediately started to plan the 2012 King's Daughters Conference. It would be bigger, better, grander and totally fitting for a real princess. Now that I know that money is no object for my Father, the King, I intend to go all the way and create a conference so magnificent that women know their worth and experience a touch from heaven. Money cannot and will not stop God's work from taking place, not in D7 Church.

It's His church, not ours. Jesus died for the church[32]. His provision for His church is perfect as long as we don't get in the way and mess it up. All you need is a zero bank balance, the audacity to take ground knowing that you have a zero bank balance and faith that God will take care of His church. It's as simple as that. So what are *you* not doing because you are worried about money?

Chapter 14
When Passion Fades

When Passion

Fades

2006 → 2007 → 2008 → 2009 → 2010 → **2011** →

Leading a church is easy when you are excited, full of energy and like King David, you are consumed with zeal for the House of God. You survive on a high and each salvation keeps you going and every life changed thrills you. Energy and passion, however, don't last forever. Tiredness does come and passion does fade into indifference. Where Sunday was once the highlight of your week, it slowly becomes the dreaded day of the week. It might take months or even years, but a season without passion will come, it has to come so that you can choose to go on not based on what you feel but on who God is.

When taking a closer look at what David said in Psalms I realised that actually I felt exactly how he did – but not in a good way – I felt eaten up. Perhaps more aptly put, eaten alive as he put it. *Because zeal for Your house has eaten me up, and the reproaches of those who reproach You have fallen on me.*

- *Psalm 69:9*

Too many times have I heard this verse quoted in a positive light, I have even used it myself to encourage people to be sold out for the cause of Christ. Only when I too felt entirely consumed and heavy with the burden of the people, did I realise that verse Psalm 69:9 might have been David's expression of exhaustion not necessarily passion.

David was the representative for the people of God in His day, and it was in that role he wrote Psalm 69 as a prayer, a plea, a desperate cry to God for help. As I read through all of Psalm 69 I related wholeheartedly, I felt David's pain and suffering as I felt my own. Jesus also quoted this verse in John 2:17 directly after he drove the money-changers out of the temple. Was Jesus perhaps fed up too?

And so I am left with the conclusion that the zeal for the House of God had indeed consumed me and that the weight of the people from my church was in fact on me. My passion for the House at first consumed me in a way that I was totally in love with the House and totally sold out to the cause of Christ. In the end, I was entirely consumed and left empty and used up by the very same people.

Church became a duty which I dragged myself out of bed to perform each Sunday. Caring for people became a part of my job description and no longer my passion. Tiredness consumed me, duty consumed me, people consumed me and my passion was gone. It had all become work, work without any joy or satisfaction. The truth is that I was tired, and not the kind of tired that even a holiday would cure. This time I had to go deeper and I had to look at my lifestyle.

Personal times of worship were even a struggle and prayer just seemed like yet another obligation. It wasn't that I didn't love God anymore, I did, very much. It was more that I didn't have the energy to love Him. Many times what should have been prayer times were times of guilt where I told God how I didn't have the energy to talk to Him. I then asked for His forgiveness and lay on my bed feeling sorry for myself.

Yes, I was eaten up by my zeal for the House, but not in the way that Jesus was, not in a way that motivated me to do something, but in a way that left me empty and lifeless. It was in this place of complete emptiness that I asked God to help me get my passion back. How I felt would not cause me to give up, this was not an option. How I felt did cause me to find it hard to continue though. I was stuck in no man's land with no desire to go forward but no desire to quit and go back either.

I knew the verse that said, *and let us not grow weary while doing good, for in due season we shall reap if we do not lose heart*[33]. It was the lose heart part that concerned me. Had I lost heart? Does this mean that I would not reap? Was all my work in vain? I began to ask myself some hard questions:

1. Was I still passionate about Jesus?

I answered yes. Jesus saved me from certain death. I knew who I was with Him and I knew who I was without Him. My gratitude for what Jesus saved me from was undeniable. I was still totally in love with my hero, the one who rescued me from the filth where I once lived.

2. Did I still believe in God?

A legitimate question that must be asked, it is not safe to assume. I had tried not to believe in God once or twice during this journey. I tried to deny Him. I was angry at

Him. I couldn't see how He could allow me to go through things I was going through. I did try and almost convinced myself that He didn't exist but I got stuck at creation. I can never get past creation, there is no way that this amazing planet with all its intricacies and details and beauty could have just appeared. Someone must have created it. I could not deny God, even when I wanted to, because creation is evidence of a Creator.

3. Was I still willing to live and die for the cause of Christ?

When asking myself this question directly I was surprised that there was still a yes in my heart. Strangely enough I could find nothing else that was worth living or dying for. If I was going to suffer it had to be for this one thing and this one thing only. Even though I was exhausted and wanted a break, I could still honestly say yes to this question. I did not want to quit I just wanted a good long break.

4. Did I still see the vision God had given us for D7 Church?

At times no. At times yes. Perhaps it was sometimes hope and sometimes faith. The thing is, if I didn't see the vision then there was no point. Everything else seemed too small to strive for, too possible and too easy. I had to believe in the mammoth vision God had given us, to believe in anything less would mean that I didn't need God, I could do it on my own. I doubted and had weak, discouraging moments, but all things considered, I still saw the vision and still wanted to live trying to do my part to bring it about.

5. Did I still love the people?

That one was a little tougher. The word 'people' just made me cringe — I immediately imagined a bucket of leaches being chucked on me to suck the life out of me. What a disgusting thought, but that is what the word people made me feel!

But, as I put faces and names to the word 'people' my heart softened a little. I saw the precious people that I truly did love. Some of them I wanted to shake and tell them to wake up, others I wanted to write off and never see again. Even though I thought this at first, considering their faces long enough made me feel compassion for them. Did I still love the people? Deep down inside I did, I just needed a break from their needs.

6. What would life look life if I stopped doing church?

I took some time to visualise all the details. I saw myself staying home and playing with the children, cooking, cleaning and just chilling in the evening. Then I thought that looked a bit boring for a long term plan so I imagined what life would look like if I went back to work and got a regular job. Boring too. Ummm, what else could I do? Uh, church? Church was definitely the most fun thing to do with life, perhaps it would be more fun if I got paid to do it. Actually, I had more than when I had a salary and I knew that I would get a salary again one day, but this time for doing the job that I loved which was church.

7. Did I really want a life without leading a church?

Not really, perhaps not an entire life without leading a church, perhaps just little breaks. Perhaps if I had more holidays and more fun it would be more bearable. Perhaps with some adjustments I could find more balance.

And so, as much as I wanted to run away from church I realised that I didn't really want to run, what I needed was a good rest and a way to find my passion. With this in mind, I set out, with the Holy Spirit as my travel companion, to find my passion.

Passion Builders

1. Walk with Passionate People

"God please make them cancel!" This was my desperate plea to God one Friday afternoon. I sat at my computer pressing 'send and receive' over and over again waiting for an email from them saying that they couldn't make it any more. The email never came and I knew that I could not cancel, we *never* cancelled. I had no real reason to cancel; I was not sick or busy or caught up in any sort of family emergency. Cancelling was not an option, I had learned never to cancel. So, I accepted that they were definitely coming over to my home for dinner that evening.

Reluctantly, I headed to the kitchen and started preparing dinner. Candles were set at the table and everything looked really pretty as usual. All that was missing was my heart. My heart was not in it. I did not want to be around people, especially churchy people who needed to talk about church stuff. I just wanted to go to bed and watch several movies and eat pop corn – all alone!

Dave arrived a bit early, which was wonderful, he was easy to chat to and having him arrive first made the transition a little easier. Then they came. Pastors. People from another church. We sat down to dinner and within minutes we hit it off. All night we shared our stories, we shared concerns, joys, dreams and our hopes for the future. It was fantastic and when the time came for them to leave I didn't want them to go! There was so much more to talk about.

Reluctantly, I let them walk out the door to go home but everything inside of me screamed for more. One evening of chatting to other passionate people lit a fire inside of me. It seemed that almost all the passion that had died in the past few months was suddenly rekindled. I was excited about church again and I actually had hope for the rest of the journey. I can't imagine how much I would have lost out on if I had cancelled dinner and gone to bed to watch movies.

Passionate people are priceless! I could not get through the ups and downs of church life without them. Dave is one of our key passionate people, whenever we feel down in the dumps he reminds us of all the good stuff and he does it with such passion and enthusiasm. Without Dave, Eric and I would surely not have made it this far.

Passionate people are essential! Negative people are always available; they are ready to jump into action with complaints and are quick to bring you down at a moment's notice. Negative people are easy to find and they exist in every church. A sure way to destroy a church and the pastors is to allow too many negative people into your life. Passionate people are essential to keeping the balance and putting things in perspective. You need passionate people so make sure you surround yourself with them, hang out with them and if you feel particularly down like I did that one evening, force yourself to be with them.

Passionate people are not negotiable! Do not think that you are OK on your own. You cannot walk alone; it is not good and not advisable. *Two are better than one, because they have a good reward for their labour. For if they fall, one will lift up his companion. But* **woe to him who is alone** *when he falls, For he has no one to help him up. Again, if two lie down together, they will keep warm; But how can one be warm alone? Though one may be overpowered by another, two can withstand him. And a threefold cord is not quickly broken.*

-   Ecclesiastes 4:9-12

Passionate people are vital. We can fall in many ways and passion is one of them, we can get cold but with someone by our side we will be warm. I found this to be true. Passionate people are vital to our survival as church planters. Passionate people are valuable. Don't take them for granted. You will soon realise the value of their role in your life when they are no longer there. Embrace them, thank God for them and make sure you value them. Even when you don't feel like cooking for them or spending time with them, know that they are worth any effort you have to put in to keep them in your life. Take care of them, keep them close and treasure what they bring into your life. Without them your life may grow very dull and cold.

Seek out passionate people, intentionally build a friendship circle of passionate people. I have had many dinners with many people and there are a few pastoral couples from Gloucester that I never want to lose. These pastors understand our life, they feel our pain and our struggles, but they don't allow us to wallow in self-pity, they build us up, they share their passion with us, they draw out our passion that can sometimes lay dormant. If you are a church planter or a leader in any form of ministry, seek out such people and when you find them don't let them go.

Invest in your relationship with them, when you feel down they will lift you up, when you get cold they will keep you warm. They won't do it because they have to, they won't even have to make an effort. You might even be doing it for them at the same time. It's like putting together two coals that are dying in a fire. As soon as they get near each other they warm up and then burst into flame. In the same way, even if you are cold and they are cold, coming together warms all of you up. Stay close to passionate people.

2. Read with Passion

Eric and I have had seasons without many passionate people. These times have been quite cold and at times dark. Loneliness can be a reality in leadership and it is in these times that it is essential to find ways to keep your passion alive. Eric often refers to his 'mentors' but I know exactly what he is talking about. He is talking about the authors of certain books and the blogs of certain pastors that he follows. Despite years of prayer,

God had not provided the much desired mentor for Eric, so he turned to books. He read loads. He has most certainly become the man he is today largely because of the books he has read. Testimonies can build you too. Other people's stories can encourage you and give you ideas for your own church. Eric is a passionate reader and I can see how this has kept his passion alive.

I on the other hand love reading too but prefer to write. After spending many years being a book worm like Eric I now find myself writing with passion. Writing keeps my passion alive. As I spend hours trying to teach what I have learned and as I type away sharing my story, I find my passion rekindled.

Reading and writing are essential to Eric and my passion. As we mull over the words of others who have gone before us, we take comfort in knowing that we are not alone. It is easy to believe that we are the first people to have ever walked down this road. It is easy to think that we are the first people to ever have faced a particular situation. Reading greatly encourages us and teaches us about the journey we are on. At times I have agreed out loud with an author, not realising that I had become vocally involved! My heart so connected with what she said that I had to agree loudly, much to the surprise of the person sitting next to me.

I remember once while going through a passionless season Eric told me that he read of when Joyce Meyer stuck her tongue out at her own building. She wanted nothing to do with anything spiritual at all, she busied herself with cooking and cleaning and anything that was not spiritual. As Eric told me what he had read my heart leapt with the thought, "So I am not a bad person then for feeling this way! If Joyce struggled without passion then I am normal!"

Reading can restore passion. Even reading the Bible can restore passion. Sometimes it feels like the last thing you want to do. I have at times felt like reading the Bible is work and a duty, anything but a passion. Yet there is life in the Bible, it cannot be denied. The Bible is living, it is like probiotic yoghurt, it doesn't look any different from regular yoghurt, but it is because it contains live cultures that clean up your insides. *For the word of God is living and powerful, and sharper than any two-edged sword, piercing even to the division of soul and spirit, and of joints and marrow, and is a discerner of the thoughts and intents of the heart.*[34]

Eating probiotic yoghurt won't taste any different from eating yoghurt without live cultures, in fact if you don't like yoghurt you might even find it a chore to eat yoghurt. But no matter how you feel about it, it cannot be denied that it does do wonders for your insides. In the same way, the Bible is living and active and even if you have to force yourself to read just a little bit every day, it will do wonders for your 'insides'. I have seasons of passionate Bible reading and season of dry Bible reading, but I always read my Bible because I know it is good for me. I know that when I am low on passion, reading my Bible is the one thing that can give me the boost I need.

Have you ever experienced the thrill of a revelation moment? When you read something in the Bible and suddenly a light goes on inside! You see something in a new way for the first time or you totally understand what a particular verse means. It is wonderful to find the hidden mysteries in the Bible, all the things that God reveals to those who look for them. I might not always read with passion but I am passionate about reading. I know it's good for me, I know that without reading, especially the Bible, I will not grow. I may not always have the energy for a full scale Bible study but I am always passionate about the Bible just like I am a firm advocate for probiotic yoghurt.

3. Rest with Passion

One other thing that I have learned is how to rest. When we started D7 Church, Eric and I said that we will work hard and play hard, but working hard was all we did, there was little time or money for any sort of play. A similar situation cropped up in the Bible under the heading of 'Mary and Martha'! Isn't it interesting that it was the one who sat at Jesus' feet that was commended and not the one running around all stressed out from work?

Rest is a key subject in several of my books, I can't escape the importance of rest. *He Restores My Soul* is an entire book dedicated to the subject of rest and in my very first book, *Hope's Journey*, I dedicated a chapter to rest. Let me share a portion of it with you here:

Be anxious for nothing, but in everything by prayer and supplication, with thanksgiving, let your requests be made known to God; and the peace of God, which surpasses all understanding, will guard your hearts and minds through Christ Jesus.

- Philippians 4:6-7

Rest Your Mind

Heart in the original Greek text is "kardia" as mentioned in the chapter on the mind which is the thoughts or feelings of the mind.

Mind in the original Greek text is "noe ma" which means a perception, purpose, disposition or the intellect.

Would you agree with me that 'the peace of God, which surpasses all understanding,' sounds like a great rest for your mind? Paul suggests that we can have this simply by 'being anxious for nothing, but in everything by prayer and supplication, with thanksgiving, let your requests be made known to God'. Not only will this give you peace but 'will guard your hearts and minds through Christ Jesus.'

Too often I get all stressed and agitated because my 'thoughts and feelings' are filled with too much worry and so is my 'perception, purpose, disposition or the intellect'. We can rest our minds by not worrying. Um... sounds familiar? Jesus said this too several times in the Bible and clearly stated that worry can achieve absolutely nothing in our life - so why worry?

Paul brought it up again when instructing young Timothy, saying that God didn't make us worriers but gave us a sound mind. Sound mind in the original Greek means discipline or self control so accessing this sound mind involves our will. God has not given us a worried mind, He has given us a mind that we have the ability to control so we must choose to rest our minds from worry.

Rest Your Body

I have heard some people tell me not to be religious about the seventh day rest as we don't live under the law anymore. Yes, that's true, but don't throw the baby out with the bath water! I believe God gave all the instructions to the Jews for their benefit, not to catch them out with laws. If we carefully examine every single law God gave in the Old Testament, we can clearly see how they were for the Jews' benefit and still today those "tips" that God gave them are totally relevant to us too.

Why would you want to blatantly disregard God's helpful tips on how to live on planet Earth? He did create Earth and us after all. If I buy an appliance, I do like to read the manufacturer's guide to understand how to use my appliance. It would be kind of silly to throw the handbook away and then sit and struggle for weeks trying to figure out how the silly thing works, wouldn't it? In my humble opinion, I view the Bible in a similar way, as life's hand book written by the manufacturer of me.

OK, enough waffle, back to resting our bodies... God made it a very serious offence to neglect the Sabbath. He really wanted people to understand that their bodies needed rest, so he added a death clause to it as a consequence.

You shall keep the Sabbath, therefore, for it is holy to you. Everyone who profanes it shall surely be **put to death**; for whoever does any work on it, that person shall be cut off from among his people. Work shall be done for six days, but the seventh is the Sabbath of rest, holy to the LORD. Whoever does any work on the Sabbath day, he shall surely be put to death.

-       Exodus 31:14-15

In the Old Testament times, the Hebrew people lived, and when their life was fully spent, they died. There was no growing old and getting frail, there was no cancer or diabetes or dementia. God's plan was perfect and we were designed to live a full and blessed life until the day we die[35].

Now I don't think it's too farfetched to say that this still applies today. Have you heard the saying "worked yourself to death"? Rest is a gift from God and our bodies need it. Every seven days is a great idea too. I heard of a study done in Germany where they experimented with a ten day work weeks. People, as well as working animals, worked for a ten day cycle with one day of rest rather than a seven day cycle.

After a few months the experiment was deemed a failure as productivity dropped and health was compromised. The idea was to get more out of people and animals to make more money, but the ten day work week caused them to lose productivity as the people and the animals were too tired and became unhealthy. Need I say any more? Taking one day a week off purely to rest was a great idea, thank you God. Let's enjoy the good life that God has mapped out for us!

Rest Your Soul

He makes me to lie down in green pastures; He leads me beside the still waters. He restores my soul; He leads me in the paths of righteousness for His name's sake.

-    *Psalm 23:2-3*

Soul is from the Hebrew word nâphash which means to breathe or to be breathed upon, that is to be refreshed as if by a current of air. It is very interesting to note that when the Holy Spirit first came at Pentecost, He was referred to as a strong current of air. Perhaps the Holy Spirit can be thought of as the soul of God that mingles with our soul. In the beginning, when God brought Adam to life, He breathed into his nostrils and this is what made Adam a 'living soul'[36]. Our soul loves[37], hates[38], desires[39], can be empty[40], can have joy, can live and can die[41]. Jesus' soul was an offering for our sin and our souls either go to heaven or hell[42].

Our soul is our emotional side but it's also the real us and this part of us needs a rest too. It makes sense to take care of our souls as this is the only part of us that is going to last for eternity. Thankfully, we don't have to go to too much trouble to rest our souls; we only have to stay in step with Jesus. In Psalm 23 he says that He will make us to lie down in green pastures, He will lead us beside still waters and He restores my soul. He will do all these things if we allow Him. One thing I have observed is how people don't allow Him to do these things.

Many times I have seen God lead people to lie down in green pastures but they don't want to lie down, they want to keep busy! Eventually, God has to make them lie down, perhaps by sending discipline their way through a leader or perhaps by allowing an uncomfortable circumstance into their lives. Then they start questioning and crying out to God, "Why did You do this to me, why don't You care?" Too many of us do this to ourselves; we don't simply follow God's gentle prompting to lie down by green pastures so that He can restore our souls.

There is a time for everything under the sun and there is most certainly a time to allow God to restore your soul. If your soul is feeling weary, ask yourself if you have allowed God to make you to lie down in green pastures and lead you beside the still waters. It is such a beautiful time and place for us to go to and I constantly wonder why we try so hard to avoid it. The Hebrew word that is used for 'lead' beside still waters is nâhal which means to run with a sparkle. Isn't that a gorgeous picture? If we want to live this life beautifully the way God intended us to, we will run the race of life with sparkle and when it's time to slow down, we will lie down beside still waters to rest our souls. I just love that picture. It is so beautiful and I know that if I take some time out and willingly lie beside the still waters, I will surely sparkle again until my next time of rest.

Practically, for those of you who aren't relating to my nice allegory, this means that you have to stop your busyness from time to time. Trust that quiet inner voice that is telling you to stop or slow down. There is no shame in doing nothing from time to time. Lying down in green pastures is a Godly quality not laziness. Some of you may have set up a camp in the green pastures and refuse to move either due to laziness or fear of going back to a hectic life. You too have to move with the seasons and allow God to lead you beside still waters, so you can sparkle again. Simply say yes to God.

Say "yes, I am willing; please will You lead me beside still waters." The simple act of **acknowledging** where you are currently placed and **giving Him permission** to move you forward alongside still waters, is all it will take to get the momentum back in your life. He will gently lead you if you let Him and then your soul will be restored.

And so God led me into a season of rest when my zeal for His House literally consumed me. It was foolishness to think that I could serve God without having a passion for His House and to be perfectly honest I didn't want to.

In September of 2010 God clearly said to me to rest until the Christmas activities kicked in. I knew that if God wanted me to rest for that long that 2011 was going to be a very busy year. For some reason the months passed by very quickly and I don't recall having much rest at all.

Again, in September of 2011, directly after our very first King's Daughters Conference, I heard the same voice saying that same thing! This time I knew that if I didn't rest I would surely DIE. From the middle of September I started to wind things down. My biggest warning was not to start anything new until the New Year. It was essential that I wound up my duties for the year and allowed a reasonable period of rest. It took a great deal of determination but looking back from September 2011 I could see why God wanted me to rest in the final months of 2010.

I had narrowly escaped burnout from 2011 and was severely passionless and empty as a result. The pain of my condition caused me to take God's advice to rest a lot more seriously. It took at least six weeks to gradually wean myself off of my duties. I started by committing to refuse anything new, then I asked Eric if I could be excused from the weekly team meeting, then I excused myself from the band and then I closed the Friday night connect group we had at our home. All that remained by the end of October was my weekly Girl's Night. I loved spending time with the lovely ladies in our church, but I knew that to rest fully that had to go too.

It wasn't long before I resolved to close Girl's Night from mid November until January leaving me with nothing to attend to except my husband, children, my home and Sundays' church service. At first I felt lazy, then I felt heartless for saying no to meeting up with people, then I felt guilty but finally I started to feel at peace.

The biggest mistake we can make as church leaders is to think that things will fall apart without us. It won't, we are not indispensable at all. In fact, for many of the balls that I 'dropped', two more people rose up to catch them. It is entirely possible that leaders who won't let go of things hinder others from rising up. During my season of rest I was able to observe a whole new team of people rise up and take my place. It was simply beautiful. No longer did I feel the weight of all my work holding me down and no longer did I feel too busy to sit at Jesus' feet. Not once did I have to worry about the work I left behind and neither did I need to feel insecure about my place in the church.

Nothing mattered except that I rested and found my passion for Jesus and His church again. Without it, my work was pointless.

4. Love with Passion

Love Jesus more than the work you do for Him.

Little Faith

And immediately Jesus stretched out His hand and caught him, and said to him, "O you of little faith, why did you doubt?"

- *Matthew 14:31*

Eric was preaching one Sunday morning and as he read through the verse above, something jumped out and hit me, it was like a slap in the face or a cold bucket of water chucked over my head. It was right at that minute that everything made sense suddenly.

Peter took the brave step that no one else had taken, he stepped out of the boat and began to walk on water. He was doing what others thought was impossible. As we all know, he took his eyes off Jesus and saw the storm around him which caused him to begin to sink. I related this to my life and could easily see what I would consider the storm that would cause me to sink. But then it hit me, after Peter called out to Jesus to save him Jesus said that famous one liner, *"O you of little faith, why did you doubt?"*

Suddenly it became clear. Peter didn't have little faith to start, he didn't have little faith to get out the boat, and he didn't even have little faith to walk on water. What he did have, was little faith to finish what he started! I instantly related. Eric and I had started this journey full of faith, we were convinced church would explode and within a few short years Gloucestershire would boast its first ever mega church where thousands of lives were being changed daily. We set out with a dream, loads of energy and plenty of faith that what we imagined would quickly turn into a reality.

Time passed, the storm was raging fiercely and we doubted. We doubted whether or not we were truly called to leading a church, we doubted whether or not we had what it took, we doubted the vision and dream we had and at times we even doubted our teams ability. Doubt was actually more dominant than faith at this point so it wasn't surprising that we were sinking. Church had seemed to be sinking for ages but we could never quite figure out why. Little faith and doubt was the why so all that was left was to get back to where we started, full of faith, hope, energy, passion and a clear vision.

The Five Fold Ministry

During this season of fading passion something interesting happened and totally threw me! Eric and I were having a meal with a new pastor friend of ours. We met one Sunday while we were ministering in the park and instantly hit it off. Since that day we have loved every minute that we could get together, we inspired each other, helped each other and instantly loved each other. This particular day was no different; we were having one of our usual life changing conversations. When he said,

"You are not pastors, you are evangelists." I nearly fell of my chair.

"You have got to be joking!" I thought to myself or perhaps even said it out loud.

"Eric and I are not evangelists, we are the most introverted people I know and we shy away from people by nature. How can you say that we are evangelists?" In my mind I was thinking of the amazing J.John, now he is an evangelist of note. I get born again, again, every time I hear him speak! His messages are so powerful and compelling and no one in their right mind can resist Jesus after sitting under J. John's evangelism. No, Eric and I were definitely not like that. But then our pastor friend continued to share why he was convinced we were.

"You are always doing things that are focused on winning the lost. You yourself said that you found it easy to win the lost and that people are saved in your church every Sunday. We don't have that and we have no desire to be doing the sort of outreach things that you are doing."

Hmm, interesting, I thought, I had never seen it that way. As I was beginning to consider that maybe he was right he continued. "I am a teacher and my wife is a pastor, she knows everyone's story and is always on the phone and taking care of people. Neither she nor I *ever* do the sorts of things that are in the community and bringing in the lost. Our focus is always to teach, disciple and to take care of the flock. Occasionally people do get saved in our church but certainly not every Sunday."

Passion began to rise up inside of me. Perhaps he is right. If he is correct then that would answer a lot of questions and solve a lot of problems. Firstly, if we are evangelists then we have been praying the wrong prayer. We have been pleading with God to send us evangelists so that we can bring in the harvest but what we actually needed to pray for was pastors to care for the lost that did come in. We weren't growing due to lack of salvations, this was clearly not the problem. Our lack of growth was due to retention. People were leaving as fast as they were coming and if we were not pastors then clearly they didn't feel cared for and so moved on.

This was fascinating, perhaps if we prayed for pastors to care for the flock then we could be free to focus on bringing the flock in with confidence that they won't leave after a few weeks or months. The conversation continued as he said to us, "Pastor may be your title but it might not be your role."

Another interesting thought. All top level leaders in our church were given the title pastor but that did not automatically mean that they were a pastor. Sounds crazy but suddenly it all made sense. And so we left our friend's home with a total shift in perspective. Immediately we started analysing our pastors to see what their actual gifting was and discovered that we actually needed pastors. Our focus changed and our prayers changed and within months we appointed our new Community Pastors. They were right under our noses all the time but we failed to see where they would slot in. Never have I seen people flourish so quickly, they were most certainly the right people in the best possible position. Suddenly it all made sense, they were natural pastors and got straight into pastoring, doing all the important things that Eric and I never got around to. The change in the team and the church was remarkable and the guilt and weight was lifted off Eric and I. I say that because we did do what we knew was right, we did follow-ups, we made phone calls, we cared for people as best we could, but it wasn't something that came naturally.

To us, this took substantial effort and required a great deal of work on our part. When we didn't do it we felt guilty and the guilt motivated us to make calls or check in on people. We loved our people but we were not pastors, neither of us. This revelation might be one the most important keys we have discovered and might be one of the things that had saved our church. Just because your title is pastor doesn't mean that your gifting is to pastor, it could be any of the fivefold ministry, the sooner you find out which one you are the better things will flow.

Chapter 15
Enjoy the Ride

Enjoy the Ride

2006 → 2007 → 2008 → 2009 → 2010 → 2011 →

"This journey has challenged me to the core; it has been a total paradigm shift in my concept of what church really is, my kingdom perspectives, loving people and servanthood. I am not the same man I once was. My mindsets have been shattered. I am more mature, I have done things that I never thought I would be able to do.

*Now I know that only God can build His church,
we are merely instruments.   I have learned total
dependence on Him.   It has been challenging, thrilling
and most of all I have been having the time of my life!"*

-       *-Eric De Souza, Senior Pastor*

Rollercoaster rides are tame compared to leading a church! The key though is not to be freaked out by all the ups and downs but to enjoy the ride. When you are on the top take a moment to look out and enjoy the view. When things are on the decline just hold on for dear life, perhaps if you are brave throw your hands in the air and let out a scream. If you can't enjoy the ride you won't make it. It's essential to put fun into your journey and not to be too serious about everything. Laugh out loud. Make fun of yourself when you mess up.

*Not that I speak in regard to need, for I have
learned in whatever state I am, to be content: I know how
to be abased, and I know how to abound.   Everywhere
and in all things I have learned both to be full and to be*

hungry, both to abound and to suffer need. I can do all things through Christ who strengthens me.

- Philippians 4:11-13

Being content in whatever state you are in is an essential key to enjoying the ride. Getting stressed out when money is low can drive you insane and feeling the hurt every time one of your precious sheep leaves the sheepfold can hurt badly. Equally, getting caught up in pride and thinking that any success is yours can cripple you and so can other such sin. Balance is essential to enjoying the ride.

Planning fun is a part of our life as a church, we even pray for fun sometimes. In the early days of church planting the adrenalin of the journey seems enough to sustain you but in time tiredness does set in. Fun is what lifts you up and keeps you full of life. Laughter is essential, getting too serious is detrimental. Make opportunities to laugh, invite the team over for a funny movie, play board games together *regularly*. Eat together, play together, include others in your fun and before you know it, church is happening in a way that you never expected!

Chapter 16
Cast Your Net On The Other Side

Casting On The Other Side

2006 ➔ 2007 ➔ 2008 ➔ 2009 ➔ 2010 ➔ **2011** ➔

"I would like to say that since coming to D7 back in June I have finally found my place with God and Jesus. Not only has it inspired me to think positively about my life. Not

only have I found Jesus. But I have found new lovely
people that I am proud to call family."

-   Robin Hallé, D7 Church

I kept hearing the nagging thought that we should cast our nets on the other side. What was God saying though, where was the other side? The thought continued to plague me so I mentioned it to the team and we prayed about it but were none the wiser. Finally I suggested that we start 'fishing' in Cheltenham, which is the 'other side' of Gloucester.

What excited me most about this thought was that when Jesus told the disciples to cast their net on the other side of their boat[43] they caught so much fish that they couldn't contain them. Was God saying that this would happen to us too if we cast our nets on the other side? It did feel much like we had been fishing all night and caught nothing. Gloucester seemed dark, we worked really hard and did all we could to build our church there, but we caught very little 'fish'.

If this truly was God saying to us to cast out nets on the other side then it was fair to assume that we would finally catch loads of 'fish' and boy oh boy were we ready for that catch! If these past years had all been training and preparation for a mighty harvest then bring it on!

Their boats didn't sink and their nets didn't break. This greatly encouraged me as it said to me that when we did get all these new people in that we would cope. Excitement filled me as I realised the possibilities. We prayed for a few more weeks and then since no one had any other thoughts, we decided to test the waters.

First we had to find a venue, not one of my favourite jobs, but I remember a small pub that offered a function room for a Christian event a few years back, perhaps they would welcome us. Eric and I popped in for a visit, Eric not seeming too keen left me questioning. Well, after seeing his response to the venue I was sure this was the place. It was recently refurbished, only a few weeks prior, so everything was beautiful and brand new. Excitement grew so we took the team to have a look. They too loved the place so we began planning a test service at this new venue.   It was when we heard the price that we were even more thrilled! Everything was simply fantastic.

On the 25th September 2011 we had a test service at a gorgeous little pub in Cheltenham. There were only eleven of us; we didn't advertise it as we wanted to test the waters. All eleven unanimously said that it was fantastic, a lovely service and they were thrilled that we might be doing it again.

Haggai

Towards the end of 2011 Lorah-Kelly started getting a strong prophecy for our church from the book of Haggai. Frighteningly each date in Haggai seemed to tie[3] in with significant dates for our church too.

29 August 2011

"In the second year of King Darius, on the 28th August, the word of the LORD came by Haggai the prophet"

- *Haggai 1:1*

---

[3] A number of dates in Haggai can be crossed checked with dates in surviving Persian records and related accurately to our modern calendar.

It was ten minutes before church was about to start and I sat frantically scribbling my sermon notes. My sermon had been prepared all week but it seemed God had a change of plan! He wanted me to tell His people about sin. The message was strong and very uncomfortable, using words that I was not comfortable using from the pulpit like sin, fart and sanitary towels.

Doubt consumed me, was this truly the word of the Lord, would He want to say such things? I stood up to preach what I believed God wanted to say and was frightened all the way through about what the people were thinking of this message. My message title was, "Sin Smells Like Fart" and covered things like how we are comfortable with our own fart smell as we are familiar with it. In the same way we can become comfortable with our sin because we are familiar with it, but to God it still smells bad.

Shortly after preaching this message Lorah-Kelly brought it to my attention that the date in Haggai 1:1 was the same timing that I preached on sin in our church. King Darius was in his second year of reign and D7 Church was in its second year too. The date of my message was the 28th August and the date that the prophet Haggai addressed the people was 29th August. This was too close to disregard it as a coincidence, and so we continued to follow the timeline in Haggai to liken it to the journey of D7 Church. The similarities and accuracies of the dates were astounding!

"Thus speaks the LORD of hosts, saying: 'This people says, "The time has not come, the time that the Lord's house should be built."'"

- *Haggai 1:2*

Lorah-Kelly felt that this verse was showing the state of people's hearts in church. People said that they could not afford to rebuild the temple and at the time the people of D7 Church were often saying that we were a poor church and could not afford to do much. There was also the spiritual side in that people had a selfish attitude and preferred to put themselves first. Their own desires and comforts were more of a priority than the church. She got the feeling that most of the people were struggling with their sins but were comfortable and didn't want to deal with it.

It was blatantly obvious that our people didn't want to do the work, they were comfortable in their sin and would rather live with the consequences of their sin than the discomfort of dealing with it. And so as we continued to study Haggai we realised that our state was in fact very similar to the state of the people mentioned in Haggai.

"Is it time for you yourselves to dwell in your panelled houses, and this temple to lie in ruins?" Now therefore, thus says the Lord of hosts: "Consider your ways! "You have sown much, and bring in little; You eat, but do not have enough; You drink, but you are not filled with drink; You clothe yourselves, but no one is warm; And he who earns wages, Earns wages to put into a bag with holes."

Thus says the Lord of hosts: "Consider your ways! Go up to the mountains and bring wood and build the temple, that I may take pleasure in it and be glorified," says the Lord. "You looked for much, but indeed it came to little; and when you brought it home, I blew it away. Why?" says the Lord of hosts. "Because of My house that is in ruins, while every one of you runs to his own house. Therefore the heavens above you withhold the dew, and the earth withholds its fruit. For I called for a drought on the land and the mountains, on the grain and the new wine and the oil, on whatever the ground brings forth, on men and livestock, and on all the labour of your hands."

-   *Haggai 1:4-11*

Spiritual Renewal

Haggai wanted the people to consider how their current situation was a result of neglecting their relationship with God. Before they could rebuild the temple they needed to lay a spiritual foundation of reverence for God in their hearts. Renewal in our hearts had to be a part of building our church and taking it forward. Our team of leaders had grown weary and it was clear that the only way to move forward was to get desperate in putting God first, whatever that meant. Without His blessing on our church our work was pointless.

21 September

Then Zerubbabel, and Joshua, the high priest, with all the remnant of the people, obeyed the voice of the Lord their God, and the words of Haggai the prophet, as the Lord their God had sent him; and the people feared the presence of the Lord. Then Haggai, the Lord's messenger, spoke the Lord's message to the people, saying, "**I am with you, says the Lord**." So the Lord stirred up the spirit of Zerubbabel, governor of Judah, and the spirit of Joshua, the high priest, and the spirit of all the remnant of the people; and they came and worked on the house of the Lord of hosts, their God, on the 21st September, in the second year of King Darius.

-    *Haggai 1:12-15*

During the month of September Lorah-Kelly and Samuel started to fast and ask God to reveal any sin in their life or anything that would hold them back.   They wholeheartedly sought God for breakthrough for our church.   It was also during this time that we became unsure of our church venue and started having the nagging feeling that we should be moving the Gloucester congregation to a new venue. Change was in the air and everything seemed uncertain.

17 October

"On 17th October the word of the LORD came by Haggai the prophet, saying:"

- *Haggai 2:1*

Driving to church on Sunday morning, 16th October, Lorah-Kelly mentioned something interesting to me, she said, "Do you realise that you are preaching again and it's the next significant date in the book of Haggai, the second time the prophet spoke?"

Wow, what a coincidence, or was it? I nervously considered that God was having me speak on both dates in Haggai when it said that the prophet spoke. Not that I thought I was a prophet or anything but the thought did cross my mind that perhaps He was going to change my message again at the last minute and have me preach on something bizarre like last time.

He didn't and my planned message on submission was preached as I shared with D7 Church what God has revealed to me about the principle of submission. I shared with the church how submission is not only something for wives but that the Bible was full of guidelines for submission is any area of leadership. Examples include submission of children to parents, submission of country men to government, submission of church members to leaders and the mutual submission of church members to each other. Yield was the key word that I used to explain submission and I used a simple illustration of a roundabout to show the consequences of not being in submission. Just imagine the mess at a roundabout if some drivers had an attitude and refused to submit to the traffic law of 'yield to the right'.

And so the church was educated in the principle of submission and hopefully this fantastic principle was put into practice very willingly by all. Church continued and so did Haggai's prophecies: *"'Who is left among you who saw this temple in its former glory? And how do you see it now? In comparison with it, is this not in your eyes as nothing? Yet now be strong, Zerubbabel,' says the Lord; 'and be strong, Joshua, the high priest; and be strong, all you people of the land,' says the Lord, 'and work; for I am with you,' says the Lord of hosts. According to the word that I covenanted with you when you came out of Egypt, so My Spirit remains among you; do not fear!'*

"For thus says the Lord of hosts: 'Once more (it is a little while) I will shake heaven and earth, the sea and dry land; and I will shake all nations, and they shall come to the Desire of All Nations, and I will fill this temple with glory,' says the Lord of hosts. 'The silver is Mine, and the gold is Mine,' says the Lord of hosts. 'The glory of this latter temple shall be greater than the former,' says the Lord of hosts. 'And in this place I will give peace,' says the Lord of hosts.'''

-   Haggai 2:3-9

The journey continued and Lorah-Kelly felt that this section was highly significant. She interpreted it as a message to us saying that we should not be discouraged because things might not look as great as they used to, which was true since we had moved from a glamorous theatre into a not so glamorous community centre. The promise though was that God was with us and we should get to work with building the church. The great thing was that it also said, *"The glory of this latter temple shall be greater than the former"*.

13th November

Moving venues on 13th November most certainly tied in with this word. It definitely seemed like nothing compared to the fancy venue we had been in for the past years. On the outside it seemed like a step backwards but we were encouraged on our journey through Haggai and realised that it was indeed a step forward according to God's plan.

And so, on this day of writing, the 14th December 2011, Lorah-Kelly and I finish off our story with what is yet to come. There is a warning in our prophecy and a promise of God that we still have to look forward to. We eagerly look forward to the coming 18th December where God has something special in store for us. It is on this day, the 18th December, that we plan to launch our second D7 Church service in another town. We are casting our net to the other side and trusting that God is with us. We did not set this date according to the Haggai prophecy, we only discovered the striking significance of this date afterwards.

18th December

'Consider now from this day forward, from 18th December, from the day that the foundation of the Lord's temple was laid—consider it: Is the seed still in the barn? As yet the vine, the fig tree, the pomegranate, and the olive tree have not yielded fruit. **But from this day I will bless you.**'"

- *Haggai 2:18-19*

God's blessing is imminent for D7 Church. It seems that we have worked very hard but God has not blessed our work **yet**. We have not grown in numbers and have begged God to tell us why we lose people as easily as we win them to Him. Haggai's prophecy has made things clear to us. Sin and toleration of sin has kept our people away from God. We tried so hard to be a church full of grace where you could *come as you are*. Our quests to love and accept everyone led us to blindly ignore sin in the name of grace. But God, in His mercy, showed us the error of our way.

We look forward with great anticipation to the 18th December, the day that God promised to bless us from, the day that we obediently cast the net to the other side. *The Tale of a Church Planter*, our journey over the past years, draws to a close now but the journey continues. Keep an eye out for the next season in the life of D7 Church.

The Tale of a Church Planter is the story of our early days, the days before church really started to grow, the days when we were still finding our feet and growing our leaders. There is so much more to tell, so much more to be written and so much more to come, more than I could ever imagine. We will continue to record our journey, all the new ups and downs, all the excitement and joy, trials and tribulations and everything in between, will be faithfully recorded and reported to you in the next book in our series of our tales. Keep a look out for the next book, *The Tale of a Church Leader,* and read what happens from 2012 onwards in the life of D7 Church. The journey continues...

Conclusion

Perhaps you are considering leading a church as a career. After reading our story I am sure you can see that it is not your average, ordinary job. It could be, many pastors, ministers and reverends have quite successfully made it into a nine-to-five job that services the needs of the Christians.

Those that truly want to advance the kingdom of Heaven know that the kingdom of Heaven suffers violence, and the violent take it by force.[44] It cannot be a neatly packaged nine to five job, it is a calling and you must be chosen[45]. Most importantly, you must be born again. *Unless one is born again, he cannot see the kingdom of God.*[46] How could you possibly teach kingdom principles if you cannot see the kingdom? It is the same as a blind man trying to teach others about the colours of the rainbow or the beauty of a sunset. It's not possible.

I would love you to join those of us that have taken this calling seriously. It would be an honour to serve alongside you in this high calling. Take a minute to consider whether or not you are born again. Have you accepted Jesus as the only way to God, have you accepted that it is only through His blood, shed on the cross that you can be truly cleansed and made worthy? There is no other way, none of your good works will get you to Heaven, not even the good work of leading a church can get you into Heaven. The only way to the Father is through the Son. If you want to accept Jesus' invitation to receive His grace and mercy and be forgiven of your sins, please say the prayer that follows.

Dear Lord Jesus,

Today I want put my life right with you. I want to be free from all fear and torment. I want to give myself to you 100%. I say yes to your offer of perfect love and I gratefully receive this love now. I thank you that your death on the cross made it possible for me to be clean and to be free. I want to be born again so that I can see the kingdom of Heaven.

Please wash me clean today so I can have a brand new start. Please forgive me of all my past sins. Please fill me with your Holy Spirit. You are my Lord and Saviour now.

Amen

If you have prayed this prayer I would love to hear from you. Please get in touch at angela@d7church.co.uk

About Angela

Angela is a mother of four, executive pastor of D7 Church, author and song writer. Born in Crawley, she spent all of her childhood in South Africa and now lives in Cheltenham with her Brazilian husband, Eric.

Angela has a passion to see people reach their full potential. In particular, she has a heart to see women set free from the lies that the enemy has fed them. She has published many books which cover the issues keeping today's women from being free.

She also writes a Blog about being a 21st century princess www.kingsdaughters21.co.uk and hosts an annual UK women's conference www.kingsdaughtersconference.co.uk

Other Books *by* Angela

Hope's Journey

"There was a time when all I wanted was to die but now that I have tasted life I really don't want to die until I have truly lived!" Hope's Journey is a heart wrenching account of Angela's struggle with depression & suicide.

Hope's Journey STUDY GUIDE

We all need HOPE. Hope's Journey STUDY GUIDE is about working together to find the hope that we have lost - a practical study to help you find a healthier mental, emotional and physical life for self-study or group studies.

Secure on the Rock

Every little girl wants to know that their daddy thinks they are beautiful! As we grow older that doesn't change, we still longs to hear the words, "You are beautiful". But what if your daddy didn't call you beautiful but hurt you and did things he shouldn't?

Secure on the Rock STUDY GUIDE

We have all been through "stuff" that has robbed us of our security - it's time to take back what is rightfully ours. Secure on the Rock STUDY GUIDE is about finding security together, ideal for self-study or small group studies.

Passion & Purity

"God made us girls for extravagant, wild, imaginative, adventurous, fantastic loving!" Angela openly shares of how her search for passion ended up in adultery and how she managed to find her way back to purity.

Passion & Purity STUDY GUIDE

Is your marriage lacking 'spark'? Are you good friends but not passionate lovers? Get that spark back and live as God intended you to live - with extravagant, wild, imaginative, adventurous, fantastic loving!

Free

Living life the way it was meant to be.

There has to be more to life than this! What am I here for? What is my purpose? Who am I really? I have to find myself! Am I good enough? Who am I? "*Free*" explores all these nagging questions.

Being a Woman

"What is the true meaning of being a woman?" The heart of a woman screams to be free to love extravagantly and to live intentionally. A refreshing read with lively discussion from six women - it's NOT at all what you might think.

Money Matters

Are you tired of trying to get through each month, living only to make ends meet? Have you read all the books that promise 'seven steps to financial freedom' but lead you nowhere? Or are you someone who has plenty of money but can't find any satisfaction in life?

Money Matters has powerful, yet easy to understand principles that will radically revolutionise your view of money. Best of all you don't need a huge bank balance as a starting point, no matter what your current financial situation, whether rich, poor or anywhere in between, these principles will challenge you to the core resulting in financial freedom and a life of contentment GUARANTEED.

Money Matters is a set of three books that will completely revolutionise your finances. Starting with simple truths to lead you to financial freedom, followed by a devotional that will assist you in renewing your mind in the area of finances and finally a workbook that offers very practical guidelines along with spreadsheets and tools for calculating your budget.

Money Matters

Simple Truths Leading to Financial Freedom

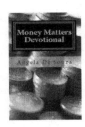

Money Matters Devotional

Renewing the Mind in the Area of Finances

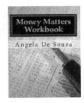

Money Matters Workbook

Sort Out Your Money One Step at a Time

References

[1] Oswald Chambers, My Utmost for His Highest

[2] Jeremiah 29:11

[3] Psalm 119:105

[4] Psalm 51:12

[5] Hebrews 13:5

[6] Exodus 20:5

[7] Psalm 46:10

[8] Ephesians 5:25

[9] 1 Corinthians 1:29

[10] 1 Timothy 3:5-6

[11] 1 Timothy 5:22

[12] Matthew 11:30

[13] Psalm 69:9

[14] Matthew 11:29

[15] Matthew 11:28

[16] From Sleepless in Seattle

[17] John 3:30

[18] Acts 17:28

[19] Ezekiel 36:26

[20] Philippians 4:13

[21] Psalm 127:1

[22] Esther 1:4

[23] Esther 1:5

[24] Esther 1:11-12

[25] Esther 1:13

[26] Esther 1:16-21

[27] Timothy 3:1

[28] Luke 12:48

[29] Luke 14:28-30

[30] Psalm 51:12

[31] Haggai 2:8

[32] Ephesians 5:25

[33] Galatians 6:9

[34] Hebrews 4:12

[35] Psalm 92:14

[36] Genesis 2:7

[37] Song of Solomon 3:3

[38] Isaiah 1:14

[39] Isaiah 26:9

[40] Isaiah 29:8

[41] Ezekiel 18:4

[42] Psalm 16:10

[43] John 21:6

[44] Matthew 11:12

[45] Matthew 22:14

[46] John 3:3

11210085R00140

Made in the USA
Charleston, SC
07 February 2012